The

AI

Selling

Revolution

The Ultimate Guide to Unlocking AI-Powered Strategies for Winning Sales

LIONEL SIM

Table of Contents

Introduction

Embracing AI for the Next Generation of Sales

T he world of sales is on the brink of a revolution, and at the heart of this transformation is Artificial Intelligence (AI). In an era where speed, personalization, and precision are key to staying ahead of the competition, AI is not just a tool for automation—it's a strategic enabler that can fundamentally change how we approach sales. This book is your guide to understanding how AI is reshaping the sales landscape, and how you can harness its power to accelerate growth, enhance customer relationships, and redefine success in your sales organization.

For decades, sales professionals have relied on intuition, experience, and hard work to close deals and build relationships. But as markets become more complex and customer expectations grow, traditional methods are no longer enough. AI offers a way to break through the noise, providing data-driven insights that allow sales teams to work smarter, not harder. By leveraging AI, salespeople can unlock new levels of efficiency, precision, and customer insight that were once out of reach.

In this book, we'll explore how AI can enhance every part of the sales cycle. From lead generation and qualification to customer engagement and closing, AI tools like predictive analytics, machine learning, and natural language processing are giving sales teams a competitive edge. With the ability to analyze vast amounts of data in real-time, AI helps identify high-potential leads, predict the best next steps in a sales process, and automate repetitive tasks—freeing up your team to focus on what matters most: building relationships and closing deals.

But AI is more than just a set of algorithms. It's a mindset. By adopting an AI-driven approach to sales, you'll not only improve the efficiency of your sales processes, but also make better decisions, anticipate customer needs, and create experiences that resonate with your audience on a deeper level. AI allows sales professionals to work with data and insights in a way that was never possible before, turning data into actionable intelligence that can predict outcomes and drive results.

As you read through this book, we will break down the practical ways AI can be implemented in your sales operations, with clear examples and case studies from companies who have already embraced this technology.

You'll learn how to incorporate AI into your sales strategy, build a data-driven sales culture, and develop a scalable approach to using AI that aligns with your business goals.

AI doesn't replace the human elements of sales—it enhances them. While automation can take care of routine tasks, AI gives your sales team the tools to engage customers in a more personalized, meaningful way. Instead of replacing jobs, AI augments the skills of salespeople, empowering them with the insights they need to make smarter decisions, build stronger relationships, and close more deals.

The sales industry is evolving, and AI is at the forefront of that change. Whether you're just starting to explore AI, or you've already begun integrating it into your operations, this book will provide you with the knowledge and practical strategies you need to stay ahead in the AI-powered future of sales.

The future is here. And it's AI-driven. Let's dive in and discover how you can leverage this powerful technology to transform your sales organization.

Chapter 1

Introduction to AI In Sales

Artificial intelligence (AI) is reshaping the sales landscape, offering unprecedented opportunities to enhance traditional practices and redefine strategies. As businesses move into this new era, understanding the role of AI becomes vital, not just for keeping up with technological advancements but for staying competitive in a dynamic market.

This chapter dives into how AI transforms sales methodologies by introducing sophisticated technologies like machine learning and natural language processing. These technologies enable businesses to conduct deep data analysis and gain insights that were once out of reach, setting the stage for more efficient decision-making processes. With AI's influence expanding, sales professionals are finding new ways to leverage technology to connect with customers more effectively and personalize interactions tailored to individual customer needs.

The journey through this chapter will illuminate how AI is being integrated within sales teams and its potential to automate routine tasks, thereby freeing up valuable time for human creativity and strategic thinking. Readers will explore real-world applications of AI, such as predictive analytics, which allow companies to foresee market trends and customer behaviors more accurately than ever before. The discussion covers AI's capability to swiftly extract meaningful patterns from extensive datasets, enhancing competitive analysis and lead prioritization.

As AI augments the dynamic between technology and human intelligence, the chapter also touches on ethical considerations and the importance of integrating AI in a manner that preserves authenticity in personal interactions. By the end of the chapter, readers will have a foundational understanding of AI's impact on sales, preparing them to navigate and harness the full potential of these innovations in modern business practices.

Defining Artificial Intelligence in The Context of Sales

In the landscape of modern sales, Artificial Intelligence (AI) has emerged as a key transformative force, poised to redefine traditional methodologies and infuse them with cutting-edge technology. Understanding this evolution begins with recognizing what AI means in a sales context and how it diverges from conventional sales strategies.

At its core, AI in sales is about leveraging advanced algorithms and computational power to process vast amounts of data swiftly and accurately. Where traditional methods might rely on manual analysis and intuition, AI excels by delving into large datasets, extracting patterns and insights that once took teams of analysts much longer to interpret. This capability allows sales professionals to make informed decisions quickly, enhancing overall strategy and execution. For instance, through natural language processing and machine learning, AI can analyze customer interactions, historical purchase behaviors, and market trends, providing predictive analytics that forecast customer needs before they become apparent.

One compelling use case is AI's ability to transcribe and evaluate sales calls using natural language processing (Source 1: Team, 2024). AI identifies customer preferences and objection patterns by dissecting conversations for tone, sentiment, and keywords, empowering sales representatives to tailor their approaches effectively during follow-up conversations. The insights drawn from these analyses offer an evidence-based foundation upon which sales strategies can be built, moving away from guesswork and intuition.

Differentiating AI from traditional techniques highlights its revolutionary impact on sales processes. Traditional sales methods often involve repetitive tasks—data entry, lead scoring, and follow-up planning—that consume valuable time and may not always yield optimal outcomes. AI, however, automates these labor-intensive activities, freeing up human resources for more strategic roles. Consider lead scoring: while traditional methods may involve ranking leads based on surface-level indicators, AI evaluates prospects through a multi-dimensional lens — assessing conversation quality, behaviors, and even social media activity. With AI, higher accuracy and efficiency are achieved, leading sales teams to focus on high-potential leads without sifting through countless low-value opportunities (Source 1: Team, 2024).

Moreover, AI introduces a new dimension to competitive analysis. In the past, sales teams would manually research competitor activities, limiting real-time responsiveness to market changes. Today, AI tools can continuously monitor competitors' digital footprints, offering timely updates on product launches, pricing shifts, and emerging marketing campaigns. This continuous stream of information enables businesses to adapt their strategies proactively, seizing opportunities and mitigating threats as they arise.

The integration of AI in sales also elevates the dynamic between AI systems and human intelligence. It's crucial to understand that AI doesn't replace the human touch in sales but complements it. AI allows human team members to concentrate on relationship-building and strategic decision-making by taking over routine tasks like scheduling meetings or generating sales reports. This synergistic relationship enhances team dynamics and productivity.

For example, AI-driven applications can generate personalized email content, ensuring communication resonates more effectively with recipients (Source 1: Team, 2024). Rather than crafting generic messages, sales representatives can focus on nurturing client relationships, creating tailored solutions, and closing deals. Meanwhile, AI helps refine sales pitches by identifying optimal timing and messaging based on comprehensive data analysis.

Another profound benefit is the augmentation of sales coaching through AI insights. Traditionally, sales coaching involved one-on-one sessions where managers provided feedback based on observations and experiences. However, with AI, sales conversations are recorded, analyzed, and reviewed for performance metrics. This data offers actionable insights into what strategies work best, allowing coaches to tailor their guidance and foster a culture of continuous improvement. Sales leaders are equipped to provide personalized coaching strategies that align with individual and team goals, driving long-term success.

These examples illustrate how AI automates processes and enhances the overall value delivered by sales teams. Yet, it is essential to approach AI adoption thoughtfully. Companies should strive to integrate AI in ways that enrich human contributions, preserve the authenticity of personal interactions, and support ethical considerations. As A I continues to evolve, sales teams must remain agile, constantly refining their skills and adapting to technological advancements.

Historical Evolution of AI in Business

In the realm of sales, artificial intelligence (AI) has emerged as a game-changer, fundamentally altering how businesses interact with consumers and streamline operations. To comprehend AI's current and future implications in sales, it's pivotal to delve into its historical roots and evolutionary path.

AI's journey within the sales sector can be traced back through a series of technological milestones that set the stage for its transformative role today. In the early days, AI wasn't directly associated with sales but included broader advancements in computer science and algorithm development. The 1990s marked one of the first significant milestones when sales processes started embracing digitalization. This era saw the advent of Customer Relationship Management (CRM) systems, which began as rudimentary databases organizing customer information. Over time, these systems transformed into comprehensive software solutions, playing a critical role in managing customer interactions. They allowed businesses to collect and analyze data more effectively, opening new avenues for increased sales efficiency.

As CRM systems evolved, they laid the groundwork for integrating AI technologies. Early implementations of AI in sales primarily focused on automating repetitive tasks and improving data management efficiency. These were exemplified by basic automation tools and rule-based systems that could execute predefined operations without human intervention. Such technology freed sales teams from mundane tasks, enabling them to concentrate on strategic areas like customer engagement and relationship building. The effectiveness of these early applications provided strong evidence of AI's potential, motivating businesses to invest in more sophisticated AI solutions.

A case study from the mid-2000s illustrates this shift well. A company that adopted early AI-driven automation tools reported a notable increase in lead conversion rates and overall customer satisfaction. Their success story became a template for other organizations looking to harness AI's power, proving that even minor incorporations of AI could yield substantial benefits.

However, the true revolution arrived with the evolution of machine learning, which marked another crucial milestone in AI's application in sales. Machine learning introduced algorithms capable of learning from vast datasets, improving themselves over time without being explicitly programmed. This self-improving nature of machine learning expanded AI's capabilities significantly beyond basic automation, breathing new life into sales strategies.

Machine learning brought forward more actionable insights and competitive advantages through advanced algorithms. It enabled predictive analytics, allowing businesses to foresee market trends and customer behavior with higher accuracy than ever before. Sales forecasting, once reliant on historical data and intuition, now benefited from real-time analysis powered by machine learning models, offering deeper insights into consumer needs and preferences.

Consider an example where a large retail company integrated machine learning into their sales processes. They analyzed shopping patterns and consumer behaviors using AI, uncovering opportunities to enhance their marketing campaigns. Personalized recommendations based on predictive analytics led to increased sales and improved customer loyalty. This illustrated how machine learning reshaped traditional sales tactics, providing an edge in the increasingly competitive marketplace.

Among the most impactful contributions of AI and machine learning is the facilitation of personalized customer experiences at scale. By analyzing past purchases, browsing habits, and demographic data, AI systems can tailor interactions to meet individual customer needs, ensuring each engagement feels curated and relevant. This personalization extends beyond recommendation engines; it influences pricing strategies, product placements, and even inventory management, all driven by AI insights.

Furthermore, AI's capacity to automate routine processes while maintaining or enhancing quality standards significantly contributes to operational efficiencies. Sales agents, for instance, gain access to AI-powered virtual assistants capable of handling customer inquiries around the clock. This ensures continuous service delivery and enhances customer satisfaction by reducing wait times. For teams already burdened with extensive workloads, AI offers relief by taking over these tasks, allowing human resources to focus on roles requiring creativity and emotional intelligence—attributes only humans possess.

As AI continues to mature, its adoption in sales is becoming not just advantageous but essential. Businesses unwilling to embrace AI risk falling behind competitors who capitalize on its benefits. However, despite its profound capabilities, AI isn't infallible. Successful implementation requires careful consideration of the organizational culture, regulatory environment, and existing technological infrastructure. While AI offers remarkable benefits, aligning its deployment with clear business objectives is crucial to maximizing its potential.

The Role of Data Analytics in AI-Driven Sales

In the dynamic world of sales, artificial intelligence (AI) is a game-changer, offering unprecedented opportunities to redefine strategies and drive business growth. Central to this transformation is data analytics, serving as the backbone for AI applications that enhance sales methodologies. By delving into how data analytics empowers AI in sales, we gain insights into the importance of quality data, the multifaceted nature of data used in analytics, and the role of advanced tools in honing sales strategies.

Data quality is the linchpin of effective AI models. High-quality data ensures more accurate forecasts and recommendations, which are vital for crafting successful sales strategies. Imagine an AI system designed to predict customer behavior; if fed with inconsistent or erroneous data, the output would be misleading, potentially derailing entire sales efforts. Therefore, maintaining stringent data standards is not just a technical requisite but a strategic imperative. Organizations must invest in robust data collection and cleansing processes to nurture a reliable foundation for AI algorithms. This entails regular audits, validation checks, and employing technologies that automate data hygiene tasks, ensuring a seamless flow of high-fidelity data from source to analysis.

The diversity of data types used in sales analytics further underscores the complexity and potential of data-driven strategies. Customer data provides insights into preferences, buying patterns, and demographics, forming the cornerstone of personalized marketing efforts. Meanwhile, operational metrics—ranging from sales cycle lengths to conversion rates—furnish actionable intelligence on process efficiencies and resource allocations. These varied data points converge to offer a holistic view of market dynamics and organizational performance, elucidating trends that might otherwise remain hidden. Sales professionals can leverage these insights to tailor their approaches, crafting narratives that resonate with target audiences and addressing specific customer pain points with precision.

Analytics tools, particularly those integrated with AI, play a pivotal role in optimizing sales strategies. Systems like lead scoring tools exemplify this integration, utilizing machine learning to prioritize leads based on their likelihood to convert. Such tools revolutionize traditional sales methodologies by enabling teams to allocate resources more effectively, ensuring that attention is concentrated on the most promising prospects. This targeted approach enhances overall efficiency and boosts conversion rates, as sales teams focus their efforts where they are most likely to succeed. The incorporation of predictive analytics extends this advantage further, equipping organizations with the ability to foresee shifts in market demand and adjust their strategies proactively.

Furthermore, analytics platforms facilitate smoother collaboration across departments, aligning marketing, sales, and customer service teams around shared objectives and insights. By providing a unified dashboard of key performance indicators and analytics-driven predictions, these tools break down silos and foster more cohesive, strategic decision-making. For example, if sales data indicates a surge in demand for a particular product type, marketing can swiftly pivot their campaigns to amplify this trend, while customer service prepares to handle increased inquiries. This synergy ensures that all facets of the organization are working towards common goals, bolstered by the latest data-driven insights.

An illustrative case of AI-powered analytics in action is its application in refining customer interactions. Personalized recommendations, informed by sophisticated AI models analyzing past purchase behaviors and preferences, significantly enhance customer satisfaction. Brands like Amazon have mastered this art, continuously improving their recommendation engines to align with evolving consumer tastes, thus driving repeat business and brand loyalty. Similarly, AI-powered chatbots can provide real-time assistance tailored to individual needs, emulating the touch of a human sales associate at scale. The ability to deliver such tailored experiences transforms customer engagements from transactional interactions into meaningful connections.

However, integrating these advanced systems with existing sales infrastructure requires careful planning and execution. Compatibility challenges must be addressed head-on, ensuring that new AI tools complement rather than disrupt established processes. Strategies to mitigate integration hurdles include conducting thorough needs assessments to identify gaps and opportunities, implementing rigorous training programs to upskill employees, and establishing pilots that demonstrate tangible benefits before full-scale rollouts. Moreover, fostering a culture of innovation within the organization encourages teams to embrace AI-enhanced methodologies with enthusiasm and creativity.

The impact of AI-infused analytics on decision- making is profound, shifting the paradigm from intuition-based judgments to data-driven strategies. In the past, sales managers might rely on gut feelings to forecast the next quarter's results. Today, AI models analyze vast datasets to provide predictions with remarkable accuracy, empowering leaders to make informed decisions that steer their companies toward success. This evolution not only optimizes internal operations but also positions organizations to better anticipate and respond to external market forces, maintaining a competitive edge in an increasingly data-centric landscape.

Bringing It All Together

This chapter has provided an insightful exploration into the fundamentals of artificial intelligence (AI) and its transformative role in modernizing sales strategies. By understanding AI's capacity to process vast data quickly, sales professionals gain tools for making informed decisions that enhance strategy and execution. Whether through predictive analytics or automation of routine tasks, AI enables a shift from traditional intuition-based methods to evidence-driven approaches. This transformation not only elevates sales efficiency but also fosters a dynamic interplay between AI systems and human intelligence, releasing professionals to focus on relational and strategic endeavors.

Moreover, the chapter underscores the evolutionary journey of AI within the sales domain, highlighting significant milestones like the integration of machine learning and the enhancement of customer experiences through personalization. As sales professionals incorporate AI applications in their strategies, they enhance their competitive advantage, adapting swiftly to market shifts. The narrative illustrates how AI is reshaping the landscape, providing nuanced insights into consumer behavior while emphasizing the importance of thoughtful adoption. Maintaining ethical considerations and preserving human interaction remain paramount as businesses continue adapting to these technological advancements, ensuring that AI's potential contributes positively to growth and success.

Chapter 2

AI Tools Transforming Sales

A I tools are transforming sales by reshaping traditional methods and introducing innovative solutions that drive both efficiency and effectiveness. As the digital era progresses, businesses need to adapt their strategies to keep pace with technological advancements that influence customer interactions and overall sales performance. AI in sales is not just a futuristic concept; it's a reality that's reshaping how sales teams operate, allowing them to predict trends, understand customer behavior deeply, and automate various tasks that once required significant human effort.

This changing landscape offers an exciting opportunity for sales professionals to enhance their approaches, ensuring they remain competitive and relevant in a rapidly evolving market.

In exploring the intersection of AI and sales, this chapter delves into a range of A I tools that are making significant impacts in the field. The chapter covers the breadth of AI applications available today, from AI- powered Customer Relationship Management (CRM) systems that leverage data analysis to optimize customer interactions to sophisticated lead scoring solutions that prioritize prospects with high conversion potential. It also examines how these tools provide real-time insights and analytics, allowing sales teams to adapt quickly to changing market demands.

Furthermore, readers will discover the role of chatbots and virtual assistants in enhancing customer experiences and improving internal productivity within sales organizations. By understanding these AI-driven transformations, sales professionals can better position themselves for success in a technology-driven world.

Overview of Popular AI Sales Tools

Artificial Intelligence (AI) is revolutionizing sales processes by providing innovative tools that enhance efficiency and effectiveness. One of the most impactful applications of AI in sales is Customer Relationship Management (CRM) systems. These systems leverage AI to improve customer interactions, analyze data trends, and automate communication strategies. For sales teams, this means shifting from reactive customer service to a more proactive approach.

AI-powered CRMs can analyze vast amounts of customer interaction data, identifying trends and patterns that may not be obvious to human eyes. For instance, they can track customer preferences, purchase history, and engagement levels over time, allowing sales professionals to tailor their engagements strategically. This personalization not only improves customer satisfaction but also enhances the likelihood of conversion, as communications are more relevant and timely. Moreover, automation within CRM systems facilitates routine tasks such as follow-up emails, appointment scheduling, and feedback gathering. These automations free up valuable time for sales reps, enabling them to focus on building stronger relationships with high-potential clients and developing strategic initiatives to drive sales growth.

Lead Scoring Solutions represent another transformative AI tool in sales. These solutions employ sophisticated algorithms to prioritize leads based on their likelihood of conversion. By AI can determine which leads are most promising by analyzing variables such as engagement history, behaviors, and demographic data. This data-driven approach eliminates guesswork, ensuring that sales teams allocate their resources effectively to engage prospects who exhibit the highest potential for conversion. For example, a company using AI-driven lead scoring might discover that leads engaging frequently with educational content are more likely to convert. By concentrating efforts on nurturing these specific leads, sales teams can optimize their strategies, resulting in improved conversion rates and a higher return on investment.

Beyond prioritizing leads, AI tools provide real-time insights that empower sales professionals to adapt quickly to changing market conditions or customer needs. The ability to access dynamic data on-demand means that sales teams can make informed decisions, anticipate client requirements, and respond with agility. This adaptability is crucial in maintaining a competitive edge in an ever-evolving marketplace.

Chatbots and Virtual Assistants are enhancing customer experiences by handling routine inquiries and tasks through natural language processing. These AI tools simulate human conversation and can assist customers around the clock, addressing common questions, guiding them through processes, or even helping with purchases. By providing immediate responses, they significantly reduce wait times and improve overall customer satisfaction. Consider a scenario where a customer needs assistance outside regular business hours; chatbots can step in to provide answers or escalate issues to human agents when necessary, ensuring seamless support continuity.

Virtual assistants are not limited to just customer-facing roles; they also play an integral role internally within sales organizations. By managing schedules, setting reminders, and providing quick access to critical information, they enhance the productivity of sales reps. Consequently, sales professionals can devote more energy to complex decision-making and creative problem-solving, rather than administrative duties.

Implementing AI tools in sales not only boosts operational efficiency but also paves the way for a deeper understanding of customer needs. When AI systems compile data from diverse sources such as social media interactions, email correspondence, and purchase histories, they construct comprehensive customer profiles. These profiles enable sales teams to craft highly personalized pitches and offerings, aligning perfectly with individual customer preferences and expectations. Personalized approaches built on robust data analytics foster stronger customer relationships and increase the potential for long-term loyalty.

The advantages of AI in sales extend beyond immediate transactional benefits to broader strategic gains. With AI, businesses can identify emerging trends before they become opportunities or threats. Predictive analytics equip sales leaders with foresight into future market dynamics, enabling proactive adjustments in sales strategies. For example, an AI system might predict a surge in demand for certain products during a particular season, prompting timely inventory and marketing strategy adjustments.

By integrating AI into sales processes, companies not only enhance their current operations but also set themselves up for sustainable growth. The shift towards AI-driven processes represents not just a technological upgrade but also a cultural transformation. Organizations embracing AI technologies exhibit a commitment to innovation, continuous learning, and adapting to new business paradigms. Such a mindset fosters resilience and positions businesses favorably in competitive landscapes.

Comparative Analysis of Leading AI Applications

In today's rapidly evolving sales landscape, the integration of AI tools has become indispensable for teams seeking to enhance efficiency and effectiveness. This section delves into some of the leading AI applications transforming the sales sphere, enabling professionals to make informed decisions that align with their strategic objectives. Our focus will be on Salesforce Einstein, HubSpot AI, Pipedrive, Zoho CRM, Gong, and Chorus—each bringing unique capabilities to the table.

Salesforce Einstein stands at the forefront with its comprehensive suite of analytics tailored for large sales teams. Known for its robust predictive lead scoring and opportunity insights, Einstein leverages advanced machine learning algorithms to help sales representatives prioritize high-potential leads and manage risks in their pipelines. Its ability to automate follow-up actions and provide next-best action recommendations is particularly advantageous for large teams managing extensive client databases. This tool's strength lies in its seamless integration with Salesforce CRM, which offers predictive forecasting and customer segmentation to streamline sales processes.

On the other hand, HubSpot AI caters to small businesses with its intuitive interface and user-friendly features. As a part of the acclaimed HubSpot Sales Hub, this AI tool provides invaluable support through predictive lead scoring and automated email tracking. Unlike Salesforce Einstein, which is more suited to enterprises with dedicated IT resources, HubSpot AI simplifies the experience and reduces the learning curve for smaller teams. HubSpot's conversation intelligence and sales forecasting capabilities enable small businesses to compete effectively by enhancing their relationship-building strategies and closing deals efficiently.

When comparing pipeline visualization capabilities, Pipedrive emerges as a leader with its easy-to-use, visually appealing interface designed for small to mid-sized businesses. It enables users to drag and drop deals across various stages, thereby simplifying the management of customer relationships. Pipedrive's focus on straightforward usability without sacrificing powerful analytics makes it a favorite among teams focused on straightforward sales activities. In contrast, Zoho CRM appeals to budget-conscious teams by offering a variety of functionalities at competitive price points. With deep integration capabilities and AI- powered data analysis through Zia, Zoho stands out in providing customizable sales reports and trend predictions that are accessible to teams working within tighter financial constraints.

Focusing on call analytics, Gong provides groundbreaking insights into interactions, making it a valuable asset for sales teams looking to refine their communication strategies. By transcribing calls and analyzing conversational dynamics, Gong surfaces actionable insights that can steer the direction of sales conversations toward success. The platform's ability to track sentiment and engagement further enhances a team's ability to understand and improve their customer engagement efforts.

Complementing Gong is Chorus, renowned for its emphasis on coaching feedback to foster improved sales approaches. Now part of ZoomInfo's suite, Chorus captures and analyzes customer interactions, spotlighting key highlights and extracting actionable items. Through detailed performance analytics, Chorus empowers managers to conduct effective training and identify areas where sales reps can improve. This focus on coaching sets Chorus apart as a tool designed not only to analyze but also to advance the skillset and success rate of sales personnel.

Criteria for Selecting The Right AI Tool

In the fast-paced world of sales, where technology continuously reshapes strategies and operations, choosing the right AI tools can dramatically impact success. For sales professionals navigating this landscape, understanding key criteria for evaluating these tools is crucial to aligning them with organizational objectives.

Firstly, the balance between tool functionality and usability significantly influences its effectiveness in a sales environment. An AI tool might boast advanced features, but adoption rates will likely be low if it's cumbersome to use. Sales teams thrive on speed and efficiency; therefore, a tool must not only be powerful but also intuitive enough for swift integration into daily routines. A user-friendly interface that minimizes the learning curve can lead to seamless adoption, reducing the time and resources spent on training. This balance ensures that the team spends more time leveraging the tool for its intended purpose—boosting sales—rather than grappling with its complexities.

Ensuring that an AI tool integrates seamlessly with existing systems is another vital consideration. Integration capabilities are paramount for maintaining the accuracy of data and ensuring that workflows remain uninterrupted. The last thing any sales team needs is a tool that disrupts established systems or requires painstaking manual data entry. Compatibility enhances scalability, as it enables the tool to grow alongside the business without necessitating significant overhauls or reconfigurations. To evaluate this, one can begin by assessing how the tool connects with current CRMs or marketing automation platforms, checking for features like real-time data syncing, which keep insights fresh and actionable.

Another important aspect is the cost versus value relationship. Initial costs can often be misleading if long-term benefits and efficiencies aren't factored in. While some AI tools may require a higher upfront investment, their ability to automate repetitive tasks and provide valuable insights can significantly enhance ROI over time. When assessing the financial side of AI tools, consider not just the immediate expenses but also potential hidden costs such as additional licensing fees or necessary upgrades in hardware. The true measure lies in whether the tool can drive substantial efficiency gains that justify the expenditure.

Finally, the availability of support and training resources plays a crucial role in effective implementation and continued usage of an AI tool. No matter how advanced a tool is, challenges will arise during deployment and everyday use. Having access to comprehensive training materials, webinars, and responsive customer support can mitigate these hurdles, allowing users to develop confidence and proficiency quickly. Support infrastructures, including in-app help and easy-to-access documentation, ensure that users have the assistance they need at their fingertips, promoting consistent and effective use of the tool.

Choosing the right AI tools that align with sales goals involves considering a holistic view of how these solutions will integrate and function within existing frameworks. Balancing functionality with usability ensures that teams can adopt new technologies without significant disruption.

Ensuring compatibility with current systems safeguards data accuracy and supports scalability, making transitions smoother and more efficient. Evaluating cost versus value helps anticipate long-term benefits, turning initial investments into strategic assets. Finally, robust support and training resources underpin successful implementation, enabling users to fully leverage the tool's potential.

Final Insights

In this chapter, we've delved into how AI tools are transforming sales through enhanced efficiency and effectiveness. By examining the capabilities of AI-driven CRM systems, lead-scoring solutions, chatbots, and virtual assistants, we've highlighted their role in reshaping customer interactions and refining sales strategies. These tools help sales teams move from a reactive to a proactive approach, providing data-driven insights that guide decision-making. They automate routine tasks, freeing up time for more strategic initiatives, while also personalizing customer engagements to boost satisfaction and conversion rates. The integration of AI not only streamlines operations but also fosters a deeper understanding of customer needs, enabling more tailored and impactful communication.

Furthermore, the comparative analysis of leading AI applications such as Salesforce Einstein, HubSpot AI, Pipedrive, Zoho CRM, Gong, and Chorus illustrates the diverse functionalities these tools offer to meet different business requirements. Understanding the criteria for selecting the right AI tool is essential for aligning it with organizational objectives. Factors like usability, integration capabilities, cost versus value, and access to support and training resources play crucial roles in successful implementation. As we continue to embrace AI technologies, it's clear that businesses equipped with the right AI tools can navigate the evolving sales landscape more effectively, fostering sustainable growth and staying competitive.

Chapter 3

Integrating AI into Your Sales Strategy

I ntegrating AI into your sales strategy is a transformative venture that promises to redefine how businesses approach their sales processes. Artificial intelligence introduces tools and techniques that streamline operations, offering new levels of efficiency and precision in targeting the right audience. Sales professionals who adopt A I enable their companies to stay competitive in a rapidly evolving market. This chapter delves deep into how such technology can be seamlessly incorporated into existing sales frameworks, enhancing not only the performance of sales teams but also the overall business growth potential.

Within this chapter, readers will explore various practical strategies for effectively embedding AI into sales practices. The discussion covers aligning sales objectives with cutting-edge AI capabilities, ensuring businesses effectively target desired outcomes. By mapping out the most relevant AI features—like predictive analytics and CRM systems—to optimize sales conversion rates, organizations can prioritize high-quality leads. Furthermore, the text emphasizes establishing robust frameworks that smoothly accommodate AI tools within current sales processes. This integration minimizes disruptions and fosters a synergistic relationship between human expertise and AI-driven insights. Readers will also learn about the importance of continuous evaluation and feedback mechanisms in keeping AI strategies attuned to dynamic sales environments. Equipped with these insights, sales and marketing professionals can confidently leverage AI to drive substantial improvements in both efficiency and customer satisfaction.

Mapping AI Capabilities to Sales Objectives

Integrating AI into your sales strategy successfully depends on aligning AI tools with clearly defined sales objectives. This begins with identifying primary sales goals, such as increasing lead conversions or enhancing customer engagement. By understanding these key objectives, businesses can trategically deploy AI to target desired outcomes more effectively. For instance, if boosting lead conversion rates is a top priority, AI-powered CRM systems and predictive analytics can analyze and prioritize high-quality leads, enabling sales teams to focus their efforts on prospects with the best potential for conversion.

Once core sales goals are set, comparing the features of various AI tools becomes critical. Predictive analytics, machine learning algorithms, and conversational AI are just a few examples of technologies that offer unique benefits when strategically aligned with sales objectives. Predictive analytics, for instance, can forecast future trends based on historical data, providing sales teams with insights to make informed decisions. By selecting AI features that align with specific sales outcomes, companies can ensure that their technology investments directly support their strategic goals.

Developing a comprehensive framework is essential to guarantee that AI solutions consistently match sales objectives. This involves integrating AI tools in a way that they work seamlessly with existing sales processes, thereby enhancing rather than disrupting operations. A practical approach might involve setting up dashboards that track performance metrics in real-time, giving sales teams immediate feedback on how well AI tools are supporting their goals. By continuously monitoring these metrics, organizations can evaluate whether their AI investments are yielding the expected results and identify areas for improvement.

Creating a robust framework also means being open to adjustments based on performance metrics. As sales landscapes evolve, so too must the AI tools and strategies deployed. Performance metrics and KPIs should be regularly reviewed to assess the effectiveness of AI solutions in meeting sales goals. Suppose a particular AI tool isn't delivering the anticipated improvements in customer engagement; in that case, businesses should be ready to pivot their approach or incorporate additional data sources to enhance AI outputs. Regularly updating AI models ensures they remain relevant and effective in the dynamic sales environment.

Incorporating feedback loops is another pivotal strategy for maintaining alignment between AI and sales targets. Feedback loops enable continuous improvement by collecting data from sales interactions, customer feedback, and market changes, which inform the recalibration of AI systems. For example, if an AI system designed to optimize customer engagement notices a dip in interaction quality, it can flag this issue for human analysis and fine-tuning. This iterative process helps refine AI models, ensuring they keep pace with evolving business needs and market conditions.

A practical guideline for implementing feedback loops involves establishing clear channels for communication between AI systems and sales teams. Sales staff should have easy access to AI-driven insights and feel empowered to provide feedback on the relevance and accuracy of these insights. Businesses can create a synergistic relationship that enhances overall sales performance by fostering a collaborative environment where human expertise and AI capabilities coexist.

Moreover, it's crucial to stay informed about advancements in AI technology to maintain a competitive edge. With AI rapidly evolving, keeping abreast of new developments allows sales teams to leverage the latest tools and techniques for optimized outcomes. Training programs and workshops can help sales professionals understand how to effectively implement AI, ensuring they are equipped to utilize these tools to their fullest potential.

To navigate challenges and seize opportunities presented by AI integration, businesses should adopt a mindset shift. Rather than viewing AI as a replacement for human roles, it should be seen as a partner that augments human capabilities. This perspective encourages sales teams to embrace AI as a valuable resource that enhances efficiency and decision-making. Collaborative intelligence, where AI handles data analysis, and humans manage emotional interactions, creates a balance that leads to more insightful and personalized customer experiences.

Lastly, measuring the success of AI integration involves both quantitative and qualitative assessments. Quantitative metrics, such as increased conversion rates and improved customer satisfaction scores, provide tangible evidence of AI's impact. Qualitative feedback from sales teams and customers offers insights into the AI experience, highlighting strengths and areas for enhancement. Celebrating achievements and recognizing the role of AI in reaching sales milestones boosts morale and reinforces the value of AI integration.

Creating Synergy between Human and AI Efforts

In today's dynamic sales environment, the balance between human intuition and artificial intelligence (AI) capabilities is crucial in crafting a robust sales strategy. AI brings unprecedented accuracy and speed to data analysis, enhancing decision-making processes with profound insights. Yet, while AI offers these analytical marvels, it cannot replicate the human ability to connect emotionally, build relationships, or exercise intuition during interactions with clients. This synergy between man and machine ensures that sales strategies are both informed by data and enriched by personal touch.

Recognizing complementary strengths between AI and humans is fundamental to effectively integrating AI into sales strategies. AI analyses vast datasets, uncovers patterns, and segments customer profiles based on buying intent or potential engagement. Its capacity to manage repetitive tasks like initial lead qualification allows sales teams to focus on nurturing client relationships and understanding nuanced customer needs, an area where human skills shine. As such, using AI for predictive analytics to tailor customer interactions frees sales professionals to dedicate their expertise to empathetic and intuitive engagements (AI's Impact on Modern Sales Strategies, 2023).

Integrating AI also requires thoughtful design of team structures that leverage technology for efficiency. By letting

AI handle routine lead assignments, sales managers empower their reps to concentrate on converting high-potential leads into loyal customers. Efficient lead distribution minimizes downtime and ensures leads are promptly attended to, increasing the likelihood of successful transactions. In this setup, AI acts as the backbone of the operations, facilitating a streamlined process that ultimately enhances productivity and morale among sales representatives.

Training is another critical component when embedding AI into sales practices. Sales teams need guidance and resources to comprehend how evolving technologies can aid their objectives. Training programs should emphasize AI as a supportive tool rather than a replacement, helping teams understand its role in augmenting their work. By familiarizing them with the basics of AI functionalities, sales teams can become more adept at interpreting AI-generated data to refine their strategies and improve interpersonal communications with clients. Continuous education keeps the team updated with advancements, ensuring they maintain a competitive edge in leveraging AI solutions effectively (Wilson & Daugherty, 2018).

Moreover, establishing clear communication channels and shared language around AI metrics is imperative for fostering teamwork and trust within sales teams. When everyone speaks the same 'AI language,' collaboration becomes seamless, with each member understanding precisely what the data represents and how it impacts strategy. Regular meetings and workshops can be instrumental in building a cohesive approach to AI integration, addressing concerns, explaining new findings, and honing shared goals. Open dialogue encourages transparency, allowing teams to discuss potential ethical concerns related to data privacy and ensuring AI tools align with customer expectations and regulatory requirements.

Developing an AI Integration Roadmap

Incorporating artificial intelligence (AI) into sales processes can dramatically transform the way businesses operate, delivering increased efficiency and productivity. To begin effectively integrating AI, it's crucial to first conduct a current state analysis of existing sales practices. This involves examining how your current sales strategies function and identifying areas where AI could fill gaps or enhance performance.

For instance, analyzing customer interactions can highlight areas ripe for automation. AI can streamline lead qualification by automating repetitive tasks such as data entry and follow-ups. According to insights from Source 1, automation not only speeds up these processes but also reduces errors and enhances forecasting accuracy. By scrutinizing these aspects, one can identify potential enhancements that AI integration would bring, ultimately leading to a more efficient sales process (*AI Sales Forecasting in 2024: Your Guide to More Profitable Pipelines*, 2024).

Following a thorough analysis, setting clear milestones becomes essential for phased implementation. Establishing small, achievable goals will help manage the project's scope and keep the team motivated. Breaking the integration into manageable phases allows for controlled progress and gives room to address any unforeseen challenges. For example, start with implementing

AI tools for basic tasks such as data organization before moving on to complex applications like predictive analytics. This step-by-step approach ensures that changes are systematically incorporated without overwhelming the team or disrupting daily operations.

Moreover, embedding feedback loops within the integration process is pivotal for success. Feedback loops provide vital opportunities for dynamic adjustments, ensuring that the AI systems evolve along with organizational needs. Incorporating feedback during all phases allows both AI models and team workflows to be fine-tuned continuously. For example, once AI tools are deployed for handling customer queries through chatbots, collecting user feedback can guide necessary refinements. A robust feedback mechanism enriches AI training and keeps team members engaged, fostering an environment of continuous learning and adaptation.

To measure the success of AI integration, utilizing quantitative metrics offers clear insight into the effectiveness of the newly implemented strategies. Metrics could include the number of successful lead conversions, time savings, and error reductions achieved post-implementation. These figures demonstrate where A I has contributed positively, guiding further adoption strategies. Celebrating these achievements, regardless of their scale, is vital. Recognizing wins bolsters morale and reaffirms the team's capability to adapt to technological shifts, thereby encouraging a culture of innovation and continuous improvement.

One compelling case study reveals the benefits of integrating AI into sales strategies. Consider a retail business that traditionally struggled with upselling due to manual processing constraints. With AI- integrated systems, they were able to automate identification of upsell opportunities by analyzing customer buying signals. This change led to a marked increase in average transaction value and allowed sales representatives to adjust forecasts upward—reflecting higher revenue potential per customer (*AI Sales Forecasting in 2024: Your Guide to More Profitable Pipelines*, 2024). Such examples underscore the transformative impact of AI on sales strategies.

Beyond immediate sales improvements, integrating AI can also position businesses for long-term growth by enabling more strategic decision-making. With AI tools supporting data-driven insights, sales teams can better understand and predict market trends. This empowers organizations to make informed decisions, leading to more precise targeting of marketing efforts and optimized resource allocation. Firms that embrace AI-driven analytics often outperform competitors who rely solely on intuition and traditional methods, as they leverage detailed insights to anticipate shifts in consumer behavior and demand.

The narrative around AI often centers on its potential to replace human jobs. However, when strategically integrated into sales processes, AI acts more as an augmentative force that complements human capabilities. By automating routine tasks, AI elevates sales professionals' roles, allowing them to focus on what truly matters: building relationships and crafting personalized customer experiences. Instead of diminishing the need for human input, AI frees up valuable resources so that sales teams can devote more energy to creative problem-solving and strategic planning.

Implementing AI successfully involves collaboration across various departments. All stakeholders must be aligned on the objectives and anticipated outcomes. Open communication and ongoing education about AI capabilities are key in overcoming resistance and nurturing acceptance. Training sessions and workshops can demystify AI technologies, illustrating their role as allies rather than adversaries. Encouraging knowledge sharing and cross-functional collaboration can also unlock innovative approaches to leveraging AI, driving enhanced sales outcomes.

The path to effective AI integration may present challenges, requiring an organization-wide commitment to innovation and adaptability. Yet, the strategic integration of AI into sales processes promises unparalleled advantages that extend beyond efficiency gains. It opens avenues for exploring new markets and customer segments, driving competitive advantage. Companies willing to embrace this shift stand to not only optimize their sales operations but also redefine their future scope in a rapidly evolving digital landscape.

Bringing It All Together

In this chapter, we've delved into the practical integration of artificial intelligence within existing sales processes to boost their effectiveness and efficiency. We've explored how aligning AI tools with well-defined sales objectives can help businesses target desired outcomes more strategically. By deploying technologies like predictive analytics and machine learning algorithms in support of core sales goals, companies ensure that their AI investments bolster strategic aims without disrupting operations. Moreover, the adoption of comprehensive frameworks and feedback loops aids in maintaining alignment between AI functionalities and evolving sales targets, fostering continuous enhancement and adaptability.

Moving forward, understanding the synergy between AI capabilities and human expertise emerges as essential. AI excels at managing data analysis and repetitive tasks, freeing sales teams to focus on nurturing customer relationships through intuition and empathy. Setting clear communication channels and encouraging collaboration between AI systems and sales personnel amplifies the benefits, creating a balanced environment where both AI-driven insights and human judgment thrive. As sales professionals equip themselves with knowledge about advancing AI tools, they enhance their capacity to leverage these developments for improved sales strategies, anchoring their efforts in well-informed decision-making that drives business growth.

CHAPTER 4

Data-Driven Sales Techniques

D ata-driven sales techniques have revolutionized how businesses approach selling, shifting from intuition-based decisions to strategies grounded in precise data analysis. The integration of big data and AI into sales operations allows companies to harness massive volumes of information, shaping strategies that are not only informed but also dynamically adaptable to market changes. This pivot towards data-centric approaches is a response to the complex landscape of modern commerce, where consumer preferences can shift rapidly and unpredictably. Sales teams equipped with relevant data insights can anticipate needs and tailor their tactics to align perfectly with emerging trends, setting a new standard for achieving sales excellence.

In this chapter, we will delve into the specifics of how data analytics and AI are leveraged to refine sales strategies. First, we explore the process of integrating various data sources to create a comprehensive view of consumer behavior and preferences. This includes examining the combination of internal CRM data with external social media insights to craft more personalized and effective sales tactics. Additionally, we discuss the importance of data cleansing to ensure accuracy in analytics and predictions. We also look at how visualization tools transform raw data into actionable strategies by making complex datasets easily comprehensible. Finally, the chapter highlights the role of AI in enhancing predictive capabilities, allowing businesses to forecast future developments and optimize their efforts accordingly. Through these discussions, readers will gain a deeper understanding of the methodologies that empower sales teams to operate with greater precision and confidence in the digital age.

Harnessing Big Data for Sales Insights

In the evolving landscape of sales and marketing, big data emerges as a transformative force, offering invaluable insights into consumer behavior and market dynamics. Leveraging this vast ocean of data allows businesses to uncover patterns that would otherwise remain hidden, making it a critical component in crafting effective sales strategies.

One of the pivotal strategies for harnessing big data involves the integration of internal CRM systems with external social media insights. Organizations gain a holistic view of their customers' behaviors and preferences by doing so. Internal CRM data, encompassing customer interactions, purchase history, and service feedback, provides a solid foundation of personalized client information. When blended with social media analytics — capturing trends, sentiments, and real-time engagement — companies can decode the nuanced tapestry of public perception and emerging market trends. This fusion enables businesses to tailor their communications and offerings precisely, enhancing customer satisfaction and loyalty. For instance, a retail company might discover through Twitter analysis that its products are gaining traction among a younger demographic, prompting it to adjust its marketing campaigns to focus on this newfound audience segment.

Data cleansing serves as an essential process in ensuring the reliability of the insights gained from big data. The sheer volume of data collected can often include inaccuracies or irrelevant information, leading to skewed analyses. Data cleansing involves removing duplicates, correcting errors, and standardizing datasets, thus eliminating noise and boosting the accuracy of predictions. This meticulous preparation step is vital for filtering out erroneous inputs that could compromise decision-making. Consider a digital marketing agency analyzing web traffic; misleading spikes caused by bots rather than genuine user interest could derail campaign strategies without cleansing. A guideline to follow during data cleansing includes implementing automated tools to consistently scrub data before any analysis, ensuring high-quality inputs at all times.

Once the data is clean and ready for interpretation, visualization tools play a crucial role in making complex datasets comprehensible. Tools like dashboards, graphs, and charts transform dense numerical insights into visual narratives that stakeholders can easily digest and act upon. Effective data visualization not only highlights key trends but also supports faster decision-making processes. For example, sales teams can utilize visual representations of geographic sales distribution to identify underperforming regions quickly, thereby reallocating resources to areas with untapped potential. Moreover, the use of interactive dashboards allows users to drill down into specific datasets, uncovering deeper insights with a few clicks.

In addition to static reports, real-time visualization has become increasingly important in today's fast-paced business environment. With markets changing rapidly, having access to up-to-the-minute data visuals ensures that decisions are based on the latest intelligence. For example, real-time tracking of social media mentions, or website activity can alert a business to immediate issues with a product launch, allowing it to pivot strategies swiftly. A practical guideline here is to leverage platforms that offer real-time dashboard features, ensuring your team is always equipped with the freshest data interpretations to guide their actions.

Implementing these strategies effectively transforms big data from a buzzword into a practical tool that drives sales success. As data-driven cultures take root within organizations, they empower teams to be more proactive and predictive, leading to enhanced performance outcomes. The democratization of data — giving various departments access to critical insights — further promotes collaboration and innovation, fostering an environment where data backs every strategic move.

Moreover, the inclusion of AI and machine learning within this ecosystem supercharges the ability of companies to process and analyze large volumes of data efficiently. Machine learning algorithms can identify patterns at scales beyond human capability, offering predictive insights that once seemed unattainable. For instance, by analyzing past purchase patterns alongside current social trends, AI can forecast future buying behaviors, enabling sales teams to anticipate customer needs before they even arise. Businesses must embrace these technologies smartly, balancing innovative approaches with ethical considerations surrounding data privacy and security.

Predictive Analytics in Sales Forecasting

Predictive analytics has emerged as a vital tool for sales forecasting, offering businesses the means to improve accuracy and make informed resource allocations. By analyzing historical sales data, predictive models can illuminate patterns and trends that are crucial for future planning. This approach moves past traditional methods, which often rely on static data and human intuition, by incorporating advanced algorithms and machine learning to more effectively process vast amounts of data.

To begin with, building predictive models using historical sales data allows businesses to identify trends that inform future forecasts. For instance, a company might analyze several years of sales data to uncover seasonal peaks and valleys. These insights enable more accurate predictions about when demand might surge or wane, allowing businesses to prepare accordingly. Understanding these trends is fundamental to optimizing inventory levels, staffing, and marketing efforts, ensuring that resources are deployed where they will have the most impact.

One key aspect of predictive sales forecasting is the use of scoring models to prioritize leads based on their likelihood of conversion. By assigning scores to potential customers, sales teams can focus their efforts on leads that present the highest probability of closing. This targeted approach not only enhances efficiency but also maximizes revenue potential. In practice, models might combine data from past customer interactions, demographic information, and engagement metrics to produce a lead score. For example, a high score could indicate a prospect who has previously purchased similar products, engaged with marketing content, or expressed interest through various channels. By concentrating on such high-potential leads, sales teams can streamline their workflows and allocate resources more strategically.

Furthermore, monitoring economic and industry-specific trends is essential for adapting sales strategies to align with broader market conditions. External factors like economic shifts, regulatory changes, and technological advancements can significantly impact sales performance. Therefore, integrating these considerations into predictive models helps businesses stay agile in a fast-changing environment. For instance, during economic downturns, consumer spending habits often shift, necessitating adjustments in pricing strategies or product offerings. Similarly, emerging industry trends might open up new opportunities or require companies to pivot their approaches. Organizations can refine their forecasts and better anticipate market demands by keeping a pulse on these developments.

However, while the benefits of predictive sales forecasting are clear, it's important to acknowledge the challenges that come with it. The accuracy of these forecasts hinges on the quality of the data used. Incomplete or outdated information can lead to flawed predictions, making data hygiene a critical component of the forecast development process (Boris, n.d.). Businesses must ensure that their data is clean, consistent, and comprehensive to build reliable predictive models. Additionally, driving adoption of predictive analytics within sales teams requires substantial training and support, as team members must learn to integrate these insights into their existing methodologies.

The development of predictive models follows a structured framework. Firstly, data collection involves gathering historical sales records, customer demographics, and other internal metrics, alongside external data sources such as social media sentiment and news events. Next, statistical modeling and analysis techniques are employed to uncover patterns and anomalies in the data. Linear regression, time series analysis, and machine learning algorithms like gradient boosting and random forests are commonly used methods. Once a model is developed, it is set up to generate sales forecasts, offering an overview of expected future performance and enabling businesses to adjust their strategies accordingly. This process ensures that sales forecasting is both dynamic and reflective of current market realities (https:// www.facebook.com/6senseinc, 2024).

Sales opportunity scoring provides a guideline for ensuring resource allocation efficiency. By integrating predictive scoring models, sales teams are equipped to prioritize leads based on their likelihood of conversion. This stratagem fosters a targeted approach, directing energy towards prospects with higher conversion potential and thereby optimizing the deployment of sales resources. Continuous refinement of these scoring techniques ensures sustained improvements in sales processes, facilitating more effective and efficient sales pipeline management.

Personalization Through Customer Data Mining

Harnessing customer data for personalized selling strategies is a game-changer in modern sales techniques. In an era where personalization dictates customer engagement, understanding and utilizing data can significantly impact sales effectiveness and customer satisfaction.

Data mining serves as the cornerstone for identifying unique customer preferences. By analyzing vast amounts of information from various sources, businesses can discern patterns and trends that hint at what individual customers value most. This process involves sifting through data collected from websites, social media interactions, purchase histories, and more to pinpoint specific interests and behaviors. Such insights enable marketers to craft highly targeted campaigns that resonate well with their audience. For instance, if data analysis reveals a segment of customers frequently purchasing eco-friendly products, businesses can tailor their marketing efforts to emphasize sustainability in that cohort's communication, thereby increasing the likelihood of conversion and retention.

Creating buyer personas is essential to developing effective personalized strategies. A buyer persona is a semi-fictional representation of an ideal customer, based on real data about demographics, behavior patterns, motivations, and goals. When crafted properly, these personas provide invaluable insights into customer needs and expectations, allowing businesses to anticipate and address them proactively. For example, a technological company might develop several buyer personas representing different user groups, such as tech-savvy young professionals or non-tech older adults. Each persona helps in tailoring communication strategies effectively; the former may prefer detailed technical specifications, while the latter might appreciate user-friendly guides and customer support assurances. These tailored approaches foster stronger relationships and encourage loyalty by demonstrating an understanding of individual customer needs.

Automated marketing tools play a crucial role in enhancing personalization efforts by facilitating timely and relevant customer engagement. Automation allows companies to deliver personalized content at the right moment, optimizing the interaction with each customer. Tools like Customer Relationship Management (CRM) systems, email marketing platforms, and social media automation software enable businesses to track customer behaviors and automate responses accordingly. If a customer abandons a shopping cart, automated tools can send reminder emails with personalized product recommendations, potentially recapturing lost sales opportunities. This level of engagement ensures that customers feel valued and understood, which is vital in today's competitive market landscape.

Guidelines for implementing data mining effectively are vital as they help streamline the process and maximize results. Companies should focus on collecting comprehensive data sets from multiple sources, ensuring accuracy and relevance. Employing advanced analytics tools and skilled data scientists can optimize the extraction of actionable insights. Additionally, maintaining strict data privacy standards and transparency with customers about how their data is used fosters trust and compliance with legal regulations.

Similarly, when developing buyer personas, it's essential to gather data from both qualitative and quantitative sources. Surveys, interviews, and feedback forms provide qualitative insights into customer motivations and challenges, while web analytics and past purchase data offer quantitative evidence of behavior. Regular updates to personas are necessary to reflect evolving customer preferences and market dynamics.

For personalized communication, the guideline is to maintain consistency across all channels while adapting content to suit different mediums. Email remains one of the most personalized channels due to its direct nature, but integrating insights from other interactions, like social media engagement and website visits, can bolster an omnichannel approach. Messages must remain cohesive and aligned with the overall brand voice to avoid customer confusion.

Finally, automated personalized marketing requires a robust martech infrastructure. Businesses should ensure seamless integration between their CRM systems, content management systems, and analytics tools for efficient data flow and campaign execution. Regular monitoring and optimization based on performance metrics such as open rates, click-through rates, and conversion rates are vital to maintaining successful automated campaigns.

Summary and Reflections

In this chapter, we explored how data analytics and AI are revolutionizing sales strategies by offering deep insights into consumer behavior and market dynamics. By integrating internal CRM systems with external social media insights, businesses can gain a comprehensive understanding of customer preferences. This combination allows for tailor-made communication and offerings that enhance customer loyalty. The process of data cleansing ensures accuracy in these insights, while visualization tools transform complex datasets into clear visual narratives that aid in quick decision-making. The role of real-time visualization was also highlighted, emphasizing its importance in adapting to the ever-changing business landscape swiftly.

The discussion further delved into the advantages of incorporating AI and machine learning, which supercharge data processing capabilities beyond human limits, providing predictive insights that allow sales teams to anticipate customer needs effectively. Businesses equipped with these tools can proactively shape their strategies based on future buying behaviors. By fostering a data-driven culture, organizations empower teams to collaborate efficiently and innovate, ensuring that each strategic move is backed by reliable insights. Emphasizing ethical considerations around data privacy and security remains crucial as technology integration progresses, balancing innovation with responsibility.

Chapter 5

Sales Automation with AI

S ales automation with A I is rapidly transforming how organizations handle repetitive tasks within their sales processes. By automating these repetitive activities, businesses aim to enhance both productivity and results, shifting the focus from mundane chores to strategic initiatives. The contemporary sales landscape, characterized by fast-paced changes and the need for efficiency, demands innovative solutions that free up valuable resources. Automation not only reduces manual efforts but also provides a consistent framework that minimizes errors and maximizes time management. As AI continues to advance, it opens possibilities for streamlining operations and creating more opportunities for growth and innovation. Embracing these technological advancements allows companies to stay competitive while optimizing their workflow for maximum performance.

In this chapter, readers will explore practical ways to identify tasks suitable for automation and gain insights into implementing AI-driven systems within customer relationship management (CRM) frameworks. Topics include developing frameworks to evaluate task characteristics, such as repetitiveness and rule-based structures, to pinpoint ideal candidates for automation. Additionally, the discussion highlights the importance of using data-driven strategies like predictive analysis and lead scoring to improve conversion rates and customer engagement. The chapter delves into leveraging AI capabilities to automate low-value tasks, thus allowing sales teams to concentrate on revenue-driving activities. Moreover, real-life examples shed light on the potential impacts of integrating AI into CRM systems, emphasizing improved employee morale, strategic market exploration, and the development of long-term client partnerships. The content aims to equip sales and marketing professionals with actionable knowledge and tools necessary for navigating the evolving sales domain successfully.

Identifying Tasks Suitable for Automation

In today's dynamic sales landscape, recognizing which tasks can be automated is crucial for maximizing efficiency and productivity. Firstly, it's essential to establish a framework that evaluates the characteristics of these tasks. A task suitable for automation often exhibits traits such as repetitiveness and a rule-based nature. The repetitive nature indicates that the task consistently follows the same pattern or steps every time it is performed. On the other hand, rule-based tasks adhere to predefined logic or criteria, making them ideal candidates for automation since they do not require nuanced judgment calls from team members.

Implementing this framework begins with creating a comprehensive list of all tasks within a sales process. This list should include recurring activities like data entry, email outreach, scheduling follow-ups, and updating CRM systems. For each task, assess its frequency, duration, and complexity. Tasks frequently repeating, taking considerable time, and offering minimal variation typically score high on the automation suitability scale. (Source 2: Praburam, 2024) provides a detailed five-step guide on automating repetitive tasks. According to this source, an effective automation strategy begins with identifying repetitive tasks. Sales teams are encouraged to create a task inventory that captures every activity's priority, frequency, and purpose. Utilizing time-tracking tools can also provide quantitative insights into how much time each task consumes. (Allen, 2021) highlights that approximately 40% of sales teams' time is spent on non-revenue-generating tasks. Identifying these tasks allows sales professionals to focus more on revenue-driving activities.

Once tasks have been identified, the next step involves analyzing the time spent on these tasks to uncover inefficiencies and potential bottlenecks. For instance, if a significant portion of the team's day is consumed by logging information into databases or performing manual data entry, this suggests an area ripe for automation intervention. Time-tracking data can help visualize where employees are expending effort and whether these tasks align with the team's primary goals.

An example involves using customer relationship management (CRM) software to automate logging interactions with clients. By integrating AI capabilities into CRM systems, sales teams can save countless hours otherwise spent manually entering data. This shift allows teams to concentrate their energy on cultivating relationships and closing deals rather than updating records.

The impact of focusing on low-value tasks extends beyond mere productivity costs; it affects team morale too. When monotonous and repetitive tasks bog down sales staff, there is a marked decline in job satisfaction and engagement. From an organizational perspective, this could lead to higher employee turnover rates and difficulties in attracting top talent. Automating these tasks not only alleviates the burden but also boosts morale by enabling employees to engage in more meaningful work.

For instance, consider the task of cold calling—a foundational duty in many sales roles. While important, the act of dialing numbers and leaving similar voicemails can be both mundane and taxing. AI solutions, like AI SDRs mentioned earlier, can automate prospect identification and initial outreach, allowing sales representatives to focus on crafting personalized pitches and nurturing leads that show genuine interest in the product or service offered.

By reducing the time spent on routine chores, teams are better positioned to embark on strategic endeavors that drive growth. Activities such as exploring new market segments, developing innovative sales strategies, and building long-term client partnerships become feasible as more resources become available. The transition from tactical to strategic priorities doesn't just enhance business outcomes; it also redefines the role of sales professionals in a more intellectually rewarding direction.

Establishing a task automation roadmap is vital for organizations embarking on the automation journey. This involves setting clear objectives for automation projects, defining success metrics, and ensuring alignment with overall business goals. Organizations might initially emphasize automating routine processes while gradually scaling up to embrace sophisticated AI tools that handle complex functions. Regularly reviewing and optimizing these systems ensures they meet evolving needs and contribute to sustained operational excellence.

Implementing AI in CRM Systems

In today's fast-paced sales environment, Customer Relationship Management (CRM) systems are evolving to incorporate artificial intelligence (AI) capabilities that transform how professionals manage sales processes. The fusion of AI with CRM creates a dynamic platform that not only automates mundane tasks but also enhances overall productivity and effectiveness, equipping sales and marketing teams with advanced tools for strategic decision-making.

At the forefront of this integration are AI features like smart lead scoring. This capability allows sales teams to prioritize prospects by evaluating their potential to convert based on data-driven insights. Traditional methods often rely heavily on manual assessments, which can be subjective and inconsistent. In contrast, AI-based lead scoring uses algorithms to analyze customer interactions and behavioral patterns, offering a more accurate ranking of leads. This enables sales teams to focus their efforts on high-value prospects, improving conversion rates and reducing time spent chasing unlikely leads.

Predictive analysis is another powerful feature AI brings to CRM systems. By mining historical data, AI tools can forecast future customer behaviors and trends, enabling businesses to anticipate needs and proactively tailor their strategies. For instance, companies can identify when a customer might be ready for a cross-sell or upsell opportunity based on past purchase patterns, allowing for well-timed offers that resonate with individual customers. This foresight not only drives sales growth but also enhances customer satisfaction by providing relevant, timely interactions.

Chatbots are increasingly becoming a staple in AI-integrated CRMs, revolutionizing customer service and engagement. These AI-powered virtual assistants handle routine inquiries around the clock, offering instant support and freeing up human agents to address more complex issues. With the ability to learn and improve over time, chatbots deliver consistent and accurate responses, ensuring a seamless customer experience. Moreover, they gather valuable data during interactions, contributing to a richer customer profile that aids in personalization and future engagements.

The successful integration of AI into existing CRM systems involves several practical steps that necessitate collaboration across departments, especially with IT teams. The first step is to clearly define the objectives AI will achieve within the CRM framework, aligning them with broader business goals. Understanding the specific sales processes that need automation or enhancement will guide the selection of appropriate AI technologies.

Next, it's crucial to assess the existing CRM infrastructure to determine compatibility with new AI tools. This may involve updating software or hardware components to support advanced functionalities. Engaging with IT teams from the onset ensures that technical challenges are addressed early, paving the way for a smoother integration process.

Training staff on the use of AI technologies within the CRM is equally important. Sales and marketing teams need to understand both the capabilities and limitations of these tools to leverage them effectively. Workshops and continuous learning sessions can help bridge knowledge gaps and facilitate a culture of innovation and adaptability.

Once AI is integrated, establishing clear success metrics is vital to evaluate its impact on sales performance and customer satisfaction. Improvements in lead conversion rates serve as a tangible indicator of AI's effectiveness in refining sales processes. By analyzing conversion data pre- and post-AI implementation, businesses can quantify the direct contributions of AI to revenue growth.

Customer satisfaction scores provide another critical measure of success. AI-driven CRM systems offer enhanced personalization and faster response times, directly influencing customer perceptions and satisfaction levels. Companies can track these metrics over time by conducting regular surveys and monitoring feedback, adjusting strategies to reinforce positive outcomes.

Case studies from various industries demonstrate the transformative power of AI-enhanced CRMs. A retail company, for example, might leverage predictive analytics to optimize inventory management, ensuring popular items are consistently stocked based on anticipated demand. Similarly, a financial institution could use AI-driven insights to tailor product offerings to segments of their clientele, increasing uptake and loyalty.

These practical examples highlight the multi-faceted benefits of AI integration, from streamlining operations to personalizing customer experiences. The journey, however, is not without challenges. Initial setup can be time-intensive, and organizations must be prepared for potential disruptions during the transition phase. Additionally, maintaining data integrity and security amidst increased automation is paramount, necessitating stringent cybersecurity protocols.

Streamlining Lead Management Processes

Sales automation with AI offers transformative potential, particularly in optimizing lead management to enhance pipeline efficiency. This subpoint delves into strategies and guidelines for leveraging AI in various aspects of lead management, allowing businesses to streamline processes and focus on higher-value tasks.

Firstly, automated lead capture is an essential aspect of modern sales pipelines. Techniques involving AI tools, such as natural language processing (NLP) for data extraction, can significantly enhance this process. NLP allows systems to understand and interpret human language, aiding in the swift extraction of necessary information from various sources like emails or chat interactions. This automation minimizes the manual entry of lead details, reducing errors and saving valuable time.

AI-driven systems excel at identifying high-quality leads by analyzing website traffic and other engagement metrics. For instance, using predictive analytics, AI can sift through vast amounts of data to pinpoint prospects whose behavior indicates a strong likelihood of conversion. Such insights not only prioritize efforts effectively but also ensure that sales teams engage with leads who are already partially qualified. This approach aligns marketing and sales functions, promoting synergy and improving overall pipeline efficiency (*Supercharge Your Sales Pipeline: How AI Optimizes Every Stage*, 2022).

With leads captured, the next phase—lead nurturing—comes into play. Automation here involves implementing AI-driven email sequences and crafting personalized communications tailored to individual preferences and behaviors. Personalization builds rapport with potential clients, making them feel valued and understood. Through machine learning, AI can dynamically adjust communication strategies based on real-time feedback, ensuring each interaction resonates with the prospect. For example, A/B testing can be employed to fine-tune email content, leveraging AI to analyze which versions yield the highest engagement rates.

Moreover, AI helps in segmenting leads into different categories based on their interactions and profile characteristics. This smart segmentation ensures that nurturing efforts are focused and effective. By understanding the unique needs of each segment, businesses can send messages that specifically address pain points or interests, thereby fostering deeper connections with potential customers (*Supercharge Your Sales Pipeline: How AI Optimizes Every Stage*, 2022).

Enhancing follow-up communications represents another key area where AI contributes significantly. Timely and relevant outreach is critical to maintaining engagement and moving leads through the sales funnel. AI plays a pivotal role here by utilizing algorithms that determine the optimal timing for follow-ups based on lead activity patterns. For instance, if a lead frequently visits a particular product page, AI can trigger a timely follow-up email highlighting new features or promotions related to that product.

Additionally, AI-powered chatbots offer real-time engagement opportunities that keep leads interested without requiring human intervention. These chatbots can answer common queries instantly and alert sales representatives when a conversation is potentially leading to a purchase decision. AI ensures no opportunity slips through the cracks by continuously monitoring lead interactions and providing timely nudges. This proactive approach keeps the lead engaged, increasing the likelihood of conversion (*AI for Lead Generation: How It Works + Useful Tools*, 2024).

Including guidelines for measuring lead management effectiveness when integrating AI is also crucial. Metrics such as response times, engagement rates, and conversion ratios should be regularly assessed to gauge the impact of AI implementations. Businesses might employ dashboards that consolidate data from various touchpoints, offering a holistic view of lead activities. This enables continuous optimization of strategies, ensuring that the AI systems evolve alongside changing customer behaviors and market dynamics.

Another practical application involves social media listening tools guided by AI. These tools track activities on platforms relevant to the business niche, gathering insights about market trends and consumer sentiments. By integrating these insights into the lead management strategy, companies can adapt and personalize their approaches, aligning with current demands.

Finally, incorporating AI into CRM systems streamlines the overall lead management process. AI augments CRM capabilities by offering smart lead-scoring methods and automating routine data entry tasks. This integration allows sales teams to spend more time engaging with leads rather than being bogged down by administrative duties. Such a shift not only boosts productivity but also enhances job satisfaction, as employees can focus on strategizing and building stronger client relationships.

Closing Remarks

This chapter has highlighted the significant role of automation in streamlining repetitive tasks within sales processes. Sales teams can maximise efficiency by identifying routine activities like data entry and email outreach as ideal candidates for automation. The emphasis has been on creating a structured framework to evaluate the tasks' repetitiveness and rule-based nature, aiding in informed decisions about which activities to automate. Implementing these strategies allows teams to reclaim valuable time that can be redirected towards more strategic initiatives such as nurturing client relationships and exploring new market opportunities.

Furthermore, the integration of AI into CRM systems has emerged as a transformative tool for elevating sales performance. With features like smart lead scoring and predictive analysis, AI enhances accuracy and reduces manual intervention, allowing sales professionals to prioritize high-value leads effectively. The introduction of AI-powered chatbots has also revolutionized customer service by managing routine inquiries efficiently. Overall, the chapter underscores how these technological advancements not only drive productivity but also contribute positively to team morale and customer satisfaction by enabling a focus on meaningful and high-impact tasks.

Chapter 6

Ethical Considerations in AI-Powered Sales

Exploring the ethical considerations in AI-powered sales is becoming increasingly necessary as businesses strive for efficiency and effectiveness. This chapter delves into the complex realm of responsibilities linked to AI usage in sales practices. The integration of AI has transformed how companies approach selling, offering tools that significantly enhance productivity and customer engagement. Yet, with these advancements come critical questions about privacy, fairness, and transparency—areas that demand careful attention from today's sales and marketing professionals. By leveraging AI, companies have access to an abundance of data and insights, enabling unprecedented personalization and predictive capabilities. However, they must navigate the delicate balance between harnessing these technological benefits and upholding ethical standards. The challenges posed by A I are multifaceted, encompassing issues that impact consumer trust and organizational integrity.

In this chapter, readers will encounter a thorough examination of how AI intersects with key ethical concerns within sales operations. Privacy concerns and data protection take center stage as we explore the importance of maintaining clients' confidentiality while utilizing advanced analytics to drive business growth. The chapter sheds light on the imperative for compliance with legal regulations such as GDPR and CCPA, underscoring their role in fostering trust and accountability. Alongside privacy, the discussion extends to ensuring fairness and avoiding bias in AI systems, exploring how data-driven decision-making may inadvertently perpetuate discrimination if unchecked.

Practical strategies like regular audits and inclusive datasets serve as safeguards against inequities. Additionally, the narrative addresses the pivotal topic of transparency in AI processes, advocating for open communication and explainable AI to build trust between businesses and their customers. Through these discussions, the chapter equips sales and marketing leaders with valuable insights and best practices to ethically integrate AI, ultimately empowering them to navigate the evolving landscape of digital sales responsibly.

Privacy Concerns and Data Protection

Incorporating AI into sales practices offers numerous advantages, but it also introduces challenges, notably in the realm of data privacy. Utilizing these powerful tools, sales and marketing professionals must ensure they responsibly handle customer information. The increasing reliance on data for business insights has heightened the focus on how such data is collected, stored, and used. This calls for a responsible approach to data privacy to avoid legal repercussions and build trust with customers.

To begin with, businesses need to comply with data privacy laws such as the General Data Protection Regulation (GDPR) and the California Consumer Privacy Act (CCPA). These regulations are designed to protect individuals' privacy by governing how companies collect, process, and store personal data. Non-compliance not only risks hefty fines but can severely damage a company's reputation. By adhering to these laws, companies signal their commitment to respecting customer privacy, which is crucial in building and maintaining trust in the digital age.

One essential measure to address privacy concerns is obtaining explicit customer consent before collecting any data. Transparency in data collection practices encourages customers to engage more openly, knowing that their information is being handled with care. For instance, businesses can use clear and simple language to explain why certain data is needed and how it will be used. This approach not only complies with regulatory standards but also reinforces brand integrity and enhances customer loyalty. When customers understand the value exchange—what they receive in return for their data—they are more likely to feel comfortable sharing it.

Another crucial strategy involves applying data minimization principles, which advocate for collecting only the data necessary to achieve specific goals. By limiting data collection to what is essential, companies can significantly reduce the risk of breaches and improve compliance with privacy laws. Periodic audits can help assess the necessity of collected data, ensuring that redundant or irrelevant information is not held unnecessarily long. This practice not only aligns with data protection regulations but also demonstrates a company's proactive stance on minimizing risks related to data privacy.

Moreover, implementing best practices such as regular security audits and comprehensive employee training plays a vital role in safeguarding sensitive information. Security audits help identify vulnerabilities within a system and provide opportunities to strengthen defenses against cyber threats. Meanwhile, training employees on data protection protocols ensures that they are well- equipped to handle data securely and are aware of the potential risks associated with improper data management. Educating staff about phishing attacks, insider threats, and the importance of strong password policies can further fortify an organization's data protection measures.

By embedding these practices into their operational framework, businesses can create a robust shield against potential data breaches and misuse. Regular evaluation and upgrades of security technologies are essential to counter ever-evolving cyber threats and maintain high data protection standards. Additionally, fostering a culture of accountability among employees around data handling can further enhance a company's ability to effectively protect its customers' personal information.

Ensuring Fairness and Avoiding Bias

Artificial intelligence (AI) systems have brought significant advancements to sales practices, offering tools for increased efficiency and performance. However, despite these benefits, AI systems can also introduce biases, impacting fairness in sales outcomes. Understanding and addressing these issues is crucial for businesses striving to implement ethical AI-driven sales strategies.

Identifying biases in data sources is the first step towards ensuring fairness. AI systems learn from data; if this data contains societal prejudices, the AI will likely replicate them in its outputs. For instance, data used in AI models may be sourced from historical business interactions that reflect existing biases against certain demographic groups. If unchecked, these biases can lead to skewed marketing strategies or unfair customer segmentation, harming a brand's perception. Recognizing this flaw emphasizes the need for careful scrutiny of data inputs to avoid perpetuating discrimination and guiding AI development toward equitable solutions.

Regularly auditing AI algorithms is another essential practice in combating bias. Periodic audits allow companies to inspect their AI systems for unintended discriminatory actions. These audits should assess how algorithms use data sets and identify any biases that could lead to unequal outcomes. By including diverse datasets during the development phase, companies can manufacture AI tools capable of generating more balanced predictions. This inclusive approach helps organizations deliver results that accurately represent a wide range of customers, reducing the chances of alienating potential clients through biased practices.

In addition to audits, continuous monitoring using clear fairness metrics is vital for maintaining an unbiased AI operation. Companies should establish benchmarks that define what constitutes fair treatment within their sales processes. These metrics offer a measurable way to gauge whether AI systems operate equitably and allow businesses to take proactive measures before discrepancies impact customer experiences. For example, if an AI model consistently favors particular demographics over others, adjustments can be made to rectify this imbalance. Regular monitoring helps ensure that AI systems do not deviate from established fairness standards over time.

Learning from case studies where AI bias caused harm is invaluable for developing fairer AI systems. There are numerous examples across industries where AI has produced biased results, leading to public backlash and regulatory scrutiny. Consider the notable case of gender bias in Apple's credit card system, where women received significantly lower credit limits than men with similar financial profiles. Such instances underscore the importance of human oversight and the necessity for comprehensive reviews of AI decision-making processes. By analyzing these case studies, businesses can glean insights into potential pitfalls and implement safeguards to prevent similar occurrences within their operations.

Implementing fairness measures must be accompanied by guidelines to effectively minimize bias impacts. One critical guideline involves assembling diverse teams to develop and train AI systems. Multidisciplinary teams bring varied perspectives, helping identify biases that might be overlooked by homogenous groups. Additionally, engaging stakeholders in discussions about AI transparency and accountability builds trust and facilitates collaborative problem-solving efforts. Encouraging open dialogue between AI developers, business leaders, and customers fosters a culture of fairness, ensuring all voices are considered.

Another guideline involves establishing robust feedback mechanisms from users and affected parties. Feedback loops create opportunities for continual improvement and adaptation of AI systems. Customers and employees should be empowered to report perceived biases or inequities in AI-driven processes. This dynamic exchange allows businesses to refine their algorithms based on real-world usage observations, making them more inclusive and effective over time.

Additionally, creating an environment where AI systems undergo regular updates and refinements is crucial. Technologies evolve rapidly, and staying current with innovations helps mitigate bias risks. Integrating the latest research and technological advancements ensures that AI models remain relevant and aligned with contemporary ethical standards. Companies should prioritize investing in ongoing AI training and upgrading initiatives to maintain their competitiveness while upholding fairness principles.

Ultimately, exploring AI bias and fairness necessitates a commitment to ethical responsibility. Acknowledging the potential for bias highlights a broader need for vigilance and conscious efforts to eliminate discrimination from AI-powered sales practices. Businesses that embrace these challenges and actively pursue equitable solutions position themselves as industry leaders committed to diversity, inclusion, and social justice. In doing so, they can enhance their brand reputation, strengthen customer loyalty, and contribute positively to societal progress.

Building Trust with AI Transparency

Transparent AI processes play an integral role in building trust between businesses and their customers. In the increasingly digital world, where artificial intelligence (AI) drives many sales processes, ensuring transparency is not merely a guideline but a necessity. Transparency contributes to an environment of trust and cooperation between sales teams and their clients.

To begin with, clarifying AI's role in sales alleviates customer fears. It's essential for businesses to demystify how AI tools function in the sales process. Customers may harbor apprehensions about AI, fearing lack of control or understanding over decisions that affect them. By explicitly describing AI's functions, such as how it personalizes product recommendations based on browsing history or purchase patterns, companies can ease these fears. This open communication fosters a collaborative atmosphere where both sales teams and clients feel like partners in the decision-making process.

Developing explainable AI systems is another critical aspect of transparency. Explainable AI (XAI) ensures users comprehend the rationale behind AI-generated recommendations and decisions. Users gain insights into its functioning when a system can provide details – for instance, explaining that a particular product was recommended due to past purchases. This clarity boosts user confidence in AI-driven decisions because they understand and agree with the reasoning behind them. As a result, trust in the technology increases, encouraging more engagement and acceptance from stakeholders.

Furthermore, establishing robust feedback mechanisms is crucial for transparency. Allowing customers to express concerns or dissatisfaction with AI outcomes directly informs improvements in AI models, ultimately enhancing accuracy and reliability. A structured feedback loop where users can share their experiences and insights makes them feel heard and valued, strengthening their relationship with the brand. Timely responses to feedback demonstrate accountability and commitment to improving services, thereby reinforcing stakeholder confidence.

Transparency also extends to clear policies regarding algorithm and data use. Businesses must adopt transparent practices that detail how algorithms are configured and what kind of data they leverage. By openly sharing information about the sources of AI inputs and disclosing potential conflicts of interest, organizations protect their reputation while enhancing credibility. For instance, disclosing this relationship maintains ethical standards and customer trust if an AI-powered sales tool predominantly recommends products from a particular brand due to financial incentives.

Guidelines around clear communication about AI usage are essential to achieve these objectives. Sales and marketing professionals should be trained to communicate effectively about AI tools' roles, benefits, and limitations. Providing straightforward, non-technical explanations helps demystify AI processes for customers, making them feel informed and empowered.

Additionally, developing explainable AI involves designing systems that prioritize understandable and interpretable outcomes. Incorporating user-friendly interfaces and explanatory features ensures customers can easily grasp the logic behind AI suggestions. These practices enhance transparency and promote responsible AI use across all organizational levels.

Creating effective feedback mechanisms requires establishing formal channels through which customers can voice concerns or ask questions. Dedicated support teams, regular satisfaction surveys, and interactive platforms can facilitate this exchange. Such mechanisms enable continuous learning and adaptation, helping organizations align their AI models with customer expectations and needs.

To further bolster transparency, businesses should adhere to best practices concerning algorithm and data usage. This includes regularly reviewing and updating privacy policies, conducting audits of AI systems to identify and address biases, and maintaining detailed records of data collection and utilization methods. By implementing thorough documentation procedures and ensuring access to transparency reports, companies can keep stakeholders informed about any changes in AI technologies and their implications.

Summary and Reflections

The chapter has delved into the ethical responsibilities surrounding AI in sales, emphasizing privacy, fairness, and transparency. It highlighted how businesses must navigate the intricate landscape of data privacy by adhering to regulations like GDPR and CCPA, ensuring customer trust. The necessity of explicit consent and data minimization was discussed as a means to protect personal information. Moreover, implementing regular security audits and training employees emerged as vital steps in safeguarding sensitive data. Attention was also given to identifying biases in AI systems by scrutinizing data sources and conducting algorithm audits. Companies can work towards more equitable AI outcomes through diverse and inclusive datasets, reducing discrimination and enhancing brand perception.

Transparency was explored as a cornerstone for building trust between businesses and their customers. By clearly communicating AI's role in sales processes, companies can alleviate customer apprehensions, making them feel like active participants rather than passive subjects. Explainable AI and robust feedback mechanisms ensure customers understand AI-generated decisions and have ways to express concerns, promoting continuous improvement. Transparency extends to disclosing policies around algorithms and data use, maintaining ethical standards while boosting credibility. These practices collectively guide sales and marketing professionals in ethically leveraging AI, fostering a trustful and fair relationship with their clientele.

Chapter 7

Training And Development For AI- Enhanced Sales Teams

T raining and development for AI-enhanced sales teams have become essential in today's fast-paced market. Ensuring that sales professionals are equipped with the skills and knowledge to leverage artificial intelligence can significantly enhance both individual and organizational performance. With AI playing an increasingly pivotal role in sales strategies, adapting to this technology is no longer optional but a necessity. Sales teams must not only understand AI tools but also integrate them seamlessly into their workflows to stay competitive. Creating effective training programs becomes crucial as businesses strive to align technological advancements with human capabilities.

This chapter delves into how tailored training initiatives can empower sales teams to harness the full potential of AI.

In this chapter, we will explore various aspects of designing AI training programs tailored to meet the unique needs of sales teams. We will discuss how analyzing team dynamics and customizing training sessions based on proficiency levels can lead to more engaged and effective learning experiences. The chapter also examines the importance of translating complex AI concepts into simple modules, emphasizing the balance between theory and practice. Additionally, the integration of frequent, bite-sized training sessions within regular sales meetings, along with instant feedback mechanisms, will be highlighted as pivotal strategies for maintaining continuous learning and improvement. Through collaboration between sales and IT teams, crafting a relevant curriculum, and implementing structured training schedules, this chapter guides readers towards creating an adaptable learning environment that fully leverages AI's capabilities.

Designing AI Training Programs

Creating comprehensive training programs for AI-enhanced sales teams necessitates a nuanced approach, one that considers the unique needs and strengths of sales professionals. Within this framework, an effective program begins with analyzing team dynamics to tailor training appropriately. By recognizing varied skill sets within the team, leaders can ensure that each member receives relevant instruction, increasing engagement and efficacy. Different roles within a sales team may require distinct AI tools; therefore, identifying the specific tools necessary for different functions is crucial in shaping these training programs.

Customizing training sessions based on current proficiency levels ensures that no team member is left behind or disengaged due to either redundancy or overwhelming complexity. This customization involves assessing the existing knowledge base of sales representatives and aligning it with the required competencies for leveraging AI in their daily operations. Utilizing personalized learning pathways—where AI itself can play a role in assessing strengths, weaknesses, and preferred learning styles—facilitates this tailored approach (Fuchs, 2024). Such personalization can enhance both retention of new information and practical application by making learning immediately relevant.

Crafting a curriculum that translates complex AI concepts into simple and comprehensible modules further integrates AI learning into the sales process. This balance of theory and practice is pivotal. Modules should begin with foundational theories, gradually advancing to more intricate applications as learners become comfortable. Incorporating real-world scenarios where sales representatives can apply their new skills helps bridge the gap between theory and practice. Practical exercises might include role-playing interactions using AI tools or simulated customer engagements, allowing reps to experience firsthand how AI can optimize their strategies.

To reinforce learning and maintain momentum, scheduling frequent, bite-sized training sessions integrated with regular sales meetings is vital. This strategy minimizes disruption while fostering continuous learning. Unlike traditional day-long workshops that can lead to information overload, short, focused sessions encourage ongoing education without sacrificing productivity. These sessions take advantage of the natural breaks between sales tasks, seamlessly embedding learning into the workflow. Moreover, integrating training with sales meetings highlights the immediate benefits of AI tools, directly correlating training outcomes with sales success.

An essential element in these training paradigms is feedback, which should be instant and actionable. AI technologies themselves can assist by providing immediate performance assessments during simulations or customer interactions (How AI Can Help Train Sales Teams, 2024). For instance, when a sales representative participates in an AI-driven role-play, they can receive a detailed breakdown of their performance, pinpointing areas like speech pacing or objection handling that need improvement. This feedback loop not only bolsters individual performance but also allows trainers to adjust programs dynamically, ensuring that evolving challenges are addressed promptly.

Collaboration between sales and IT teams during program design, although not encompassed within this specific subpoint, plays an indirect yet significant role by providing valuable insights into technological capabilities and limitations. Encouraging cross-departmental communication can enhance program relevance and foster a cooperative environment where both technical and sales perspectives are respected and utilized.

Upskilling Sales Representatives

In the rapidly evolving landscape of sales, the integration of artificial intelligence (AI) presents a transformative opportunity. Emphasizing continuous skill enhancement with a focus on AI applications is vital for sales teams aiming to remain competitive and effective. This approach not only equips sales professionals with technological prowess but also enriches their interaction capabilities, paving the way for improved customer engagement and business outcomes.

To begin, conducting assessments is crucial in identifying skill gaps within sales teams. These assessments can be effectively carried out through a combination of surveys, interviews, and performance metrics. Surveys provide a broad overview of the team's perceived strengths and areas needing improvement, offering insights into both individual and collective needs. Interviews, on the other hand, allow managers to delve deeper into personal experiences and challenges that sales reps face when utilizing AI tools.

Performance metrics offer an objective measure, highlighting specific areas where salespersons may struggle or excel. By triangulating this data, organizations can pinpoint precise skills that require development, ensuring training programs are both targeted and efficient.

Once skill gaps are identified, familiarizing sales reps with AI tools becomes the next step. Hands-on training sessions are essential to bridge the knowledge divide. These sessions should be designed to provide practical experience, allowing sales representatives to interact with AI tools in real-world scenarios. Additionally, mentorship systems play a pivotal role in this process. Pairing less experienced sales reps with seasoned mentors who have successfully integrated AI into their sales strategies can foster a culture of learning and collaboration. This approach not only accelerates skill acquisition but also builds confidence among team members, as they witness firsthand the tangible benefits AI can bring to their sales techniques.

Integrating soft skills development with technical training forms the backbone of successful customer interactions. While proficiency in AI tools is critical, the ability to communicate effectively and empathetically remains paramount. Soft skills training focuses on enhancing active listening, emotional intelligence, and adaptability—traits that are indispensable in understanding customer needs and building strong relationships. A balanced training program that incorporates both technical expertise and essential soft skills ensures that sales professionals are not only adept at using AI- powered insights but are also capable of translating those insights into meaningful conversations with clients.

Creating personal development plans aligned with the organization's AI strategy offers a structured path for growth and progress. Each sales representative should have a tailored plan that outlines their learning objectives, timelines, and milestones. This personalized approach acknowledges individual career aspirations and aligns them with the overarching goals of the company. Regularly reviewing these plans and celebrating achievements fosters a sense of accomplishment and motivation. Recognizing progress, whether through formal awards or informal acknowledgments, reinforces the value placed on continual learning and adaptation.

By investing in these training and development initiatives, organizations can unlock the full potential of their AI-enhanced sales teams. The ability to conduct detailed assessments, coupled with hands-on training and comprehensive development plans, equips sales professionals with the necessary tools to thrive in an AI-driven environment. Moreover, integrating technical and soft skills training ensures that sales teams are well-rounded, capable of leveraging technology while maintaining exceptional customer relationships.

The long-term benefits of such an investment extend beyond immediate sales performance. Teams that are proficient in AI applications are better positioned to anticipate and respond to emerging market trends and customer expectations. This agility translates into sustained organizational growth and resilience in the face of technological advancements. Ultimately, the commitment to continuous skill enhancement in AI applications solidifies a company's competitive edge and prepares its sales force for the challenges of tomorrow's marketplace.

Fostering a Culture of Continuous Learning

In the ever-evolving landscape of sales, integrating artificial intelligence (AI) into business strategies has become a game-changer. To harness AI's potential effectively, it is crucial to cultivate a learning environment within sales teams that adapts to technological advancements. This ensures that team members remain competitive and innovative as they navigate new tools and methods.

Promoting open communication and experience sharing among team members forms the backbone of this adaptive learning culture. In an organization where AI is utilized, knowledge is power. Encouraging open dialogue not only aids in the dissemination of information about AI tools and practices but also fosters an atmosphere where team members can freely share their successes and challenges. Regular meetings, workshops, and informal discussions provide platforms for these exchanges, allowing individuals to learn from each other's experiences. For example, a team member who has successfully used predictive analytics to pinpoint leads can share their approach, helping others replicate or refine these tactics.

Recognizing and rewarding lifelong learning through recognition programs and incentives plays a significant role in motivating team members to continually enhance their skills. As technology evolves, so must the knowledge base of any competent sales team. Organizations can establish clear pathways for professional growth by offering awards, bonuses, or public acknowledgments for those who achieve educational milestones related to AI tools and strategies. Such initiatives not only reward personal achievement but also encourage others to pursue further training. Implementing these programs signals to the team that ongoing education is both valued and essential, creating an organizational culture that prioritizes continuous improvement.

Preparing teams to stay adaptable to new AI developments requires engaging with external resources and discussions. To keep their strategies effective, sales teams must remain at the forefront of AI innovations. Encouraging participation in industry conferences, webinars, and online forums exposes team members to cutting-edge ideas and practices. By facilitating access to these resources, organizations enable their teams to anticipate changes, understand emerging tools, and apply fresh insights to their workflows.

Additionally, inviting guest speakers or organizing collaborative sessions with external experts can enrich the team's understanding and widen their perspective on how AI impacts the broader sales landscape.

Feedback mechanisms are pivotal in assessing training effectiveness and refining programs continuously. Without regular evaluations, it is challenging to determine what aspects of training are working and what needs adjustment. Soliciting feedback from team members helps identify areas of strength and opportunities for improvement. This process should be iterative, with responses informing the development of future training initiatives. Surveys, one-on-one meetings, and anonymous suggestion boxes allow team members to express their thoughts comfortably. Moreover, metrics such as increased sales performance, improved customer interactions, and proficiency with AI tools provide tangible evidence of training success. Regularly updating training content based on this feedback ensures that it remains relevant and impactful, aligning closely with the evolving needs of the sales team and the technological landscape.

Establishing a structured training schedule becomes essential as organizations strive to nurture an adaptable learning environment. Determining a training schedule that fits within the team's workflow ensures that learning does not hinder day-to-day operations. Instituting periodic refresher courses reinforces learning without overwhelming the participants, enabling them to absorb knowledge over time. These sessions can be short, focused engagements designed to solidify previous teachings or introduce small increments of new information. The incorporation of such training into daily routines makes the acquisition of

AI skills a natural part of professional life rather than an isolated endeavor.

Opting for bite-sized training sessions is particularly beneficial in this context. Short bursts of educational content can be more manageable and less intimidating, allowing team members to engage actively without feeling burdened. Microlearning, which involves delivering content in small, specific segments, caters to the modern learner's preference for quicker, more efficient consumption of information. This method is conducive to sustained engagement and retention, keeping team members motivated to continue their educational journey.

Concluding Thoughts

Equipping sales teams with the necessary skills to effectively utilize AI is central to enhancing their strategic operations. This chapter explored the foundational elements of designing AI training programs, emphasizing the importance of tailoring these programs to suit individual team member needs. By assessing existing knowledge and incorporating personalized learning pathways, organizations can ensure that all team members are equipped to leverage A I tools effectively.

Furthermore, incorporating real-world scenarios into training helps bridge the gap between theoretical concepts and practical applications, enabling sales professionals to smoothly integrate AI into their workflows.

The chapter also highlighted the significance of fostering continuous learning and adaptability within sales teams. Implementing concise training sessions integrated with regular sales meetings minimizes work disruption while promoting ongoing educational engagement. Feedback mechanisms play a crucial role in refining these programs, ensuring they remain relevant and responsive to evolving technological landscapes. Encouraging cross-departmental collaboration and open communication contributes to a comprehensive understanding of AI's capabilities, further empowering sales teams to maximize the benefits of their training. Through these efforts, organizations can position their sales teams to thrive in an increasingly AI-driven sales environment.

Chapter 8

Future Trends in AI And Sales

F uture trends in AI are reshaping the sales landscape, providing unprecedented opportunities for businesses to enhance customer interactions and streamline operations. AI-driven tools like conversational AI and chatbots are revolutionizing how businesses engage with customers by offering real-time, personalized experiences. Leveraging technologies such as natural language processing and machine learning, these systems have the capability to respond swiftly and accurately to a wide array of customer inquiries, thereby fostering deeper connections and improving satisfaction rates. Additionally, AI's 24/7 availability surpasses human limitations, ensuring global outreach without downtime, which is increasingly vital in today's interconnected marketplaces. The effectiveness of AI in addressing repetitive tasks also liberates human resources, allowing employees to concentrate on more complex issues that necessitate empathy and nuanced decision-making.

This chapter delves into the myriad ways AI advancements are influencing sales strategies, enabling professionals to better adapt to rapidly changing environments. It explores the integration of machine learning algorithms that tailor customer interactions based on extensive data analysis, creating opportunities for targeted marketing and predictive analytics that refine resource allocation. The discussion extends to the seamless collaboration between AI and existing sales platforms, enhancing team efficiency through shared insights and real-time access to customer information. Furthermore, the narrative examines the dynamic content delivery capabilities of AI that enrich customer engagement and foster brand loyalty. By evaluating these emerging trends, the chapter offers invaluable insights into leveraging AI to drive business growth and maintain competitive advantage in an evolving market.

Conversational AI and Chatbots

In the ever-evolving landscape of sales and customer interaction, conversational AI emerges as a transformative force, revolutionizing how businesses engage with their customers. At the core of this transformation is the ability of conversational AI systems to deliver real-time, personalized customer interactions. By leveraging natural language processing (NLP) and machine learning, these AI-driven tools can understand and respond to customer inquiries quickly and effectively. This personalization not only meets immediate customer needs but also crafts meaningful, lasting relationships by making customers feel valued and understood. According to recent statistics, companies using chatbots have seen a 20% increase in customer satisfaction rates (HootSuite Blog).

A significant advantage of conversational AI is its capacity for 24/7 availability. Unlike human agents who operate within scheduled shifts, AI-powered chatbots remain accessible around the clock. This constant availability allows businesses to cater to global audiences, crossing time zones without any downtime. Whether it's resolving simple queries or providing product recommendations, these AI systems ensure that customers receive support whenever they need it. One study even highlights that 62% of consumers prefer interacting with a chatbot for routine inquiries due to their speed and efficiency (Rafalski, 2023). By efficiently handling frequently asked questions (FAQs), chatbots free up human agents to focus on more complex interactions that require human empathy and decision-making.

One of the most impactful capabilities of conversational AI lies in lead qualification and nurturing. Through criteria-based filtering, AI systems assess potential leads based on predefined metrics such as engagement history, demographics, and behavior patterns. This targeted approach allows sales teams to focus their efforts on high-potential prospects, thereby enhancing conversion rates. For instance, AI tools can evaluate browsing behavior and past interactions to gauge a prospect's interest level, subsequently prioritizing those who demonstrate a strong intent to purchase. This not only streamlines the sales process but also ensures that valuable resources are invested where they are most likely to yield returns. Here, an effective guideline would be segmenting prospects into categories based on engagement levels to enhance targeting accuracy.

Furthermore, the integration of conversational AI with existing sales platforms amplifies collaboration and strategy refinement within sales teams. By facilitating seamless data transfer and insight sharing, AI systems ensure that all team members have real-time access to vital customer information and analytics. This interconnectedness allows sales professionals to develop collaborative strategies based on a comprehensive understanding of customer needs and preferences. For example, by integrating AI with Customer Relationship Management (CRM) systems, sales teams can view detailed customer profiles, including purchase history, preferences, and even sentiment analysis from previous interactions. This integration fosters informed decision-making and helps tailor marketing campaigns to resonate better with target audiences.

Additionally, conversational AI enhances customer engagement through its dynamic content delivery features.

These AI tools can generate tailored content by analysing customer interactions, such as personalized product recommendations or promotional offers. For instance, if a customer frequently browses outdoor gear, the AI system can suggest related products or offer discounts on camping equipment. This level of personalization not only increases the likelihood of conversions but also enriches the overall customer experience. The ability to dynamically adapt content based on individual interactions creates a more engaging and interactive customer journey, which leads to improved brand loyalty.

Another notable feature is the cost-effectiveness of deploying conversational AI in sales processes. Automating repetitive tasks significantly reduces operational costs while increasing productivity. With AI handling routine inquiries and initial contact touchpoints, businesses can reallocate their human resources to more strategic roles within the organization. Moreover, the scalability of AI chatbots enables them to manage numerous conversations simultaneously, allowing companies to expand their customer base without proportionally increasing staffing needs. This scalability not only supports business growth but also ensures consistent service quality regardless of demand fluctuations.

The multilingual support offered by conversational AI further broadens the horizons for businesses seeking to tap into international markets. Equipped with language recognition and translation capabilities, AI chatbots can converse with customers in their preferred languages, breaking down communication barriers. This capability proves indispensable for global brands looking to provide a seamless support experience to a diverse audience. By communicating fluently across languages, businesses not only expand their reach but also build trust and credibility with their multilingual customer base.

Machine Learning Algorithms in Sales

Machine learning algorithms have become an indispensable tool in redefining sales strategies, offering a transformative edge in how businesses approach their market. At the heart of this transformation is personalization at scale, enabled by analyzing vast datasets. With machine learning, companies can craft tailored pitches that resonate with individual customer preferences and behaviors, leading to enhanced deal closure rates.

The core advantage of these algorithms lies in their ability to process immense quantities of data swiftly and accurately. This capability allows for the creation of bespoke marketing messages and product offers that align closely with specific customer needs and desires. For instance, consider a fashion retailer utilizing machine learning to analyze browsing history, purchase patterns, and feedback. By doing so, they can recommend personalized outfits or accessories that a customer is more likely to buy, thereby increasing satisfaction and sales outcomes.

Predictive analytics, another cornerstone of machine learning applications in sales, significantly enhances forecast accuracy. By scrutinizing trends and historical data, businesses can make informed predictions about future sales potential. This information proves invaluable in optimizing resource allocation, ensuring that marketing efforts are both cost-effective and strategically targeted. Imagine a tech firm that employs predictive analytics to assess the potential success of a new gadget launch. By evaluating past product performances, customer feedback, and broader market trends, the company can better allocate resources to areas likely to yield the highest return on investment, minimizing risk and maximizing efficiency.

Moreover, machine learning algorithms excel at identifying sales opportunities through pattern detection. They can recognize upselling and cross-selling potential by analyzing customer interactions and transaction histories. The ability to pinpoint which products are often purchased together or which services complement each other allows businesses to present offers that may otherwise be overlooked. Consider an online bookstore using machine learning to suggest additional titles to customers based on their previous purchases. This not only boosts revenue but also enriches the customer experience by providing additional value through targeted suggestions.

The iterative learning process inherent in machine learning provides ongoing insights for process optimization.

Sales teams benefit from continuous feedback loops, where inefficiencies in current strategies are identified and eliminated. Through this perpetual refinement, businesses maintain agility in their sales approaches, adapting swiftly to changing market dynamics. For example, a subscription service might discover through machine learning analysis that a particular aspect of their onboarding process results in higher cancellations. Armed with this insight, they can tweak their strategies to improve retention rates, ensuring long-term business growth.

Guidelines for effective implementation of machine learning in sales should certainly be considered. For personalization at scale, it's crucial to gather comprehensive data encompassing customer demographics, behavior, and purchase history. Selecting suitable algorithms, such as collaborative filtering or content-based filtering, is pivotal for building efficient recommendation systems. Ensuring accurate model training with historical data further strengthens prediction reliability, while regular updates incorporating new data help refine recommendations continuously.

In predictive analytics, guidelines revolve around choosing the right metrics to track future trends and adjusting strategies accordingly. Data from various sources, such as sales transactions, customer feedback, and market conditions, should be aggregated and analyzed consistently. Encouraging human oversight in reviewing automated forecasts can enhance decision-making, integrating intuitive understanding with machine-derived insights.

For identifying sales opportunities, leveraging machine learning tools that specialize in pattern recognition can unveil hidden potentials within datasets. It's advisable to conduct periodic reviews of algorithm performance, aligning detected patterns with actual sales outcomes. This practice ensures models remain relevant and accurate, continually contributing to revenue growth through improved upselling and cross-selling tactics.

Lastly, refining sales processes via machine learning requires a commitment to iterative learning. Regularly evaluate key performance indicators (KPIs) like conversion rates and customer engagement levels to identify areas for improvement. Foster a culture of feedback where team members actively contribute observations and suggestions based on hands-on experiences. This collaborative approach allows machine learning models to evolve alongside human expertise, creating a robust strategy adaptable to diverse scenarios.

Integrating AI with Emerging Technologies

In today's rapidly evolving digital landscape, the collaboration of artificial intelligence (AI) with emerging technologies is transforming sales strategies dramatically. This amalgamation not only enhances sales effectiveness by providing valuable insights but also propels businesses toward more informed decision-making processes, redefining how customer interactions are managed.

The integration of AI with the Internet of Things (IoT) is a significant trend reshaping the sales domain. By enabling continuous data collection through interconnected devices, businesses gain real-time insights, crucial for crafting targeted sales strategies. For instance, IoT devices in retail environments can record and transmit customer preferences, shopping habits, and even product interaction times. When analyzed using AI algorithms, this wealth of data allows companies to predict consumer behaviors and tailor marketing campaigns that resonate with specific audiences. Such real-time insights help sales teams anticipate needs, ensuring they are well-prepared for customer interactions, resulting in increased conversion rates and stronger customer loyalty.

Furthermore, AI's collaboration with augmented reality (AR) and virtual reality (VR) technologies offers unprecedented opportunities for creating immersive marketing experiences. These technologies enable customers to interact with products in an engaging and lifelike manner before making a purchase decision. Imagine a furniture company utilizing AR to allow customers to visualize how a sofa would fit within their living room space or a car manufacturer using VR to provide potential buyers with virtual test drives. These interactive experiences forge emotional connections between consumers and brands, significantly enhancing conversion rates. The impact is twofold: not only do customers feel more confident in their purchasing decisions, but they also develop a deeper attachment to the brand, fostering long-term relationships.

Blockchain technology, coupled with AI, plays a pivotal role in building trust and transparency during substantial transactions. In an era where data privacy concerns are paramount, blockchain offers a secure and transparent way to authenticate and protect customer data. By creating immutable records of customer interactions and transactions, businesses can assure clients of both security and authenticity. This assurance is especially vital for transactions involving high-value products or services, where trust is essential for successful exchanges. Customers who feel confident about the integrity of their personal information are more likely to engage in sales transactions, ultimately enhancing the business's reputation and customer base.

One of the most compelling advantages of integrating these technologies is automating routine tasks, enabling sales teams to refocus their efforts on strategic decision-making and improving the overall customer experience. AI-powered automation can handle repetitive tasks such as data entry, scheduling, and basic customer queries, freeing up valuable time for sales professionals to concentrate on more complex interactions that require human insight and creativity. This shift ensures that sales teams are not bogged down by administrative duties, allowing them to engage with customers in meaningful ways, thus promoting a cohesive and personalized customer journey.

Consider a scenario where AI systems automatically analyze and organize vast amounts of sales data to identify patterns and trends. Sales professionals can then use this information to develop informed strategies that align with customer preferences and market demands. This streamlined approach ensures that all touchpoints along the customer journey are optimized, from initial contact to post-sale support, creating a seamless and satisfying experience for the consumer.

Moreover, the synergy between AI and other technologies fosters innovation in developing new business models. For example, subscription-based services can leverage AI to personalize offerings, predicting when a customer might need to reorder or upgrade a product. By anticipating these needs, sales teams can proactively reach out with tailored recommendations, enhancing the value proposition for the customer and increasing the likelihood of repeat business.

It's important to note that while combining AI with emerging technologies offers numerous benefits, it also comes with challenges that businesses must navigate. Implementing these technologies requires careful consideration of infrastructure, data management, and the readiness of sales teams to adapt to new tools and methodologies. Ensuring smooth integration involves training staff to effectively utilize AI-driven insights and embracing a culture of continuous learning and adaptation.

Guidelines play a crucial role here. It's essential to outline clear implementation steps, identify suitable pilot projects, and set measurable goals to evaluate the effectiveness of these technological integrations. Providing ongoing support and feedback mechanisms will further enhance the efficacy of these advancements in driving sales success.

Summary and Reflections

In this chapter, we've delved into the transformative role of conversational AI and chatbots in revolutionizing sales and customer interaction. These advanced tools leverage natural language processing and machine learning to provide real-time, personalized customer engagement, enhancing customer satisfaction and fostering lasting relationships. With around-the-clock availability, AI-powered chatbots cater to a global audience, allowing businesses to cross time zones without interruption. The ability to handle routine inquiries efficiently frees human agents to focus on complex interactions that demand empathy and nuanced decision-making. Additionally, we've explored how conversational AI aids in lead qualification, nurturing potential prospects through data-driven filtering and segmentation, amplifying conversion rates for sales teams. This chapter further highlights the integration of AI with existing sales platforms, which fosters collaboration by ensuring seamless data sharing and insight availability among team members.

Furthermore, the text examines how machine learning algorithms redefine sales approaches through personalized marketing at scale and predictive analytics. By analyzing large datasets, these algorithms craft tailored pitches and enhance forecast accuracy, enabling businesses to optimize resource allocation efficiently. Pattern recognition capabilities allow businesses to uncover sales opportunities through upselling and cross-selling strategies. The chapter also touches on the integration of AI with emerging technologies like IoT, AR, VR, and blockchain, transforming sales strategies and enriching customer experiences. Through AI-powered automation, repetitive tasks are streamlined, empowering sales teams to engage customers more effectively. As businesses navigate the integration of these technologies, this chapter serves as a guide to implementing and leveraging AI-driven tools to drive growth and innovation in sales practices.

Chapter 9

Measuring Success In AI-Driven Sales Strategies

Measuring success in AI-driven sales strategies is a multifaceted endeavor that demands both precision and adaptability. As organizations increasingly integrate artificial intelligence into their sales processes, the challenge becomes not only implementing these advanced tools but also effectively evaluating their impact. This requires an understanding that traditional performance metrics may not fully capture AI's contributions. Consequently, sales professionals need to develop new sets of measurements tailored to AI applications. By doing so, they can not only assess the current benefits of their AI initiatives but also identify areas for future improvement. It is this dynamic between innovation and evaluation that positions AI as a pivotal force in modern sales operations.

This chapter delves into the methods used to evaluate the success of AI integrations within sales procedures. Readers will explore how to tailor key performance indicators (KPIs) specifically for AI-driven strategies, ensuring they align with broader business goals. The discussion will include insights into distinguishing between traditional sales metrics and those unique to AI applications, providing a framework for comprehensive performance measurement. Through tangible examples and industry comparisons, the chapter aims to illuminate best practices and guide professionals in effectively quantifying AI's impact on sales. Additionally, the narrative will highlight the importance of using both leading and lagging indicators to gain a holistic understanding of AI effectiveness, emphasizing the balance needed for continuous growth and strategic adaptation.

Defining KPIs for AI Initiatives

In the rapidly evolving landscape of AI-driven sales strategies, the establishment of key performance indicators (KPIs) tailored specifically to AI applications is essential for measuring success. Identifying relevant KPIs involves understanding which measurements are crucial in tracking AI's performance within the sales domain. Sales professionals must first determine the primary objectives of their AI initiatives. For example, metrics like response times and interaction frequency might be prioritized if the primary goal is enhancing customer engagement. On the other hand, for projects focused on operational efficiency, process automation levels or error reduction could serve as more suitable KPIs.

Finding the right KPIs necessitates a careful examination of both business goals and the specific nature of the AI technology being employed. A predictive analytics model would need a different set of measurements compared to a natural language processing tool used in customer service. Thus, accuracy and forecasting capabilities might be significant for the former, while response quality and speed may be more relevant to the latter. This nuanced approach ensures that the chosen KPIs accurately reflect the impact of AI tools on sales processes, enabling data-driven decision-making and effective adjustments based on real-world results.

Aligning these KPIs with overall sales goals is equally pivotal, as it maintains coherence throughout the organization. When AI objectives seamlessly integrate with broader business aspirations, they can produce meaningful insights and drive strategic growth. For example, if an organization's overarching goal is to boost customer satisfaction, then AI-related KPIs should contribute directly toward that end, possibly by focusing on metrics related to personalized recommendations or improved service delivery timelines. This alignment not only illustrates the value of AI initiatives to stakeholders but also supports long-term investment and development decisions.

It's important to recognize the distinction between traditional sales metrics and those specific to AI initiatives. Traditional metrics often revolve around direct outcomes such as revenue growth or market share expansion, while AI-specific KPIs might include factors like machine learning model precision or chatbot resolution rates. By distinguishing these metrics, companies can gain clearer insights into how AI technologies are driving change and identify areas requiring further refinement.

Integrating KPIs into existing frameworks is essential for holistic performance measurement. Organizations should strive to incorporate AI-specific KPIs alongside established performance indicators to provide a comprehensive view of success. This integration allows businesses to not only track immediate results but also understand long-term implications and potential areas for enhancement. Furthermore, integrating both traditional and AI-centric KPIs ensures that AI projects remain aligned with company-wide goals without losing sight of individual program achievements.

Providing tangible examples of effective KPIs across various sales scenarios can illuminate best practices and guide organizations in developing their own measurements. For instance, a useful KPI might be the conversion rate of AI-driven product recommendations in the retail industry. If a recommendation engine suggests specific products to customers and those suggestions lead to purchases at a higher rate than non-AI suggestions, then the metric effectively demonstrates AI's value in boosting sales. Another example could be within customer service departments, where AI chatbots aim to resolve queries efficiently. A helpful KPI here might be the percentage of inquiries successfully handled by bots without needing human intervention, indicating the AI system's efficacy in improving service quality and reducing workload on staff. Setting quantifiable targets within these KPIs can help maintain focus and track progress over time.

Establishing clear benchmarks allows teams to assess whether AI deployments achieve desired outcomes, providing the basis for ongoing refinement and optimization. These targets should be realistic, measurable, and directly linked to strategic objectives, ensuring they act as a reliable gauge of success.

To facilitate this, organizations can look to benchmark against industry standards. Comparing their performance indicators against competitors or sector averages offers valuable context and helps organizations understand where they stand in relation to peers. Industry comparisons can highlight strengths and weaknesses in AI integration, guiding future decisions and fostering competitive advantage.

Another key consideration is balancing leading and lagging indicators. Incorporating both types provides a more rounded picture of AI effectiveness. Leading indicators, such as the number of predictive insights generated or early engagement signals from customers, can offer foresight into potential trends or issues. Meanwhile, lagging indicators, like actual sales figures or customer satisfaction scores post-interaction, confirm the realized impacts of AI interventions. Together, these measurements enable a full cycle of assessment and continuous improvement.

Success stories of KPI implementation offer real-world illustrations of effective strategy execution. While the specifics might vary across industries, common themes include increased efficiency, enhanced customer experiences, and stronger alignment between AI operations and broader corporate ambitions. These narratives demonstrate the transformative potential of thoughtfully selected and implemented KPIs, acting as both inspiration and guidance for other organizations embarking on similar journeys.

Quantifying Improvements in Sales Performance

To effectively measure the improvements AI tools bring to sales performance, it's essential to start with a comprehensive before-and-after analysis of sales metrics. This approach involves establishing a clear baseline, which serves as a reference point for evaluating subsequent changes. Before implementing AI, gather data on key performance indicators such as sales volume, lead conversion rates, and customer acquisition costs. These metrics should provide a snapshot of current performance levels. After integrating AI, revisit these indicators regularly to detect shifts and trends. This method offers quantifiable evidence of AI's impact, helping identify areas where it has enhanced efficiency, accuracy, or customer engagement.

It's also important to attribute sales increases directly to AI interventions by addressing potential confounding factors. Controlled studies can be immensely beneficial in this regard. Businesses can draw more definitive conclusions about AI's role in performance improvements by creating test groups that use AI tools and control groups that operate without them. This strategy minimizes external influences and allows for more precise measurements of AI's effectiveness. Controlled experiments make it easier to isolate variables and pinpoint which aspects of AI contribute most significantly to sales growth, thereby providing actionable insights for future implementations.

Customer feedback is another vital component in assessing AI-driven enhancements in sales. Gathering input from clients before and after AI adoption helps gauge satisfaction levels and the perceived quality of service. Tools like surveys and interviews can capture valuable qualitative data, offering insights into how customers experience interactions powered by AI. Feedback focusing on speed, personalization, and overall experience can highlight gaps or strengths in the deployment, enabling organizations to refine strategies accordingly. Customer perceptions often serve as an indirect measure of success, illustrating not just quantitative growth but qualitative improvement in customer relations.

Moreover, real-world examples serve as powerful illustrations of AI's tangible effects on sales processes. Consider the case of OpenLending, which faced challenges in complex sales dialogues due to fluctuating economic conditions. By utilizing Quantified.ai's Sales Simulator, the company achieved a nearly 14% improvement in their sales cycle progression. This technology provided a platform for rigorous training, allowing sales reps to better handle high-stakes conversations. Such examples underscore how AI-driven tools accelerate processes and enrich sales teams' skill sets, leading to higher efficiency and effectiveness.

Similarly, T-Mobile's experience using Salesforce Einstein showcases AI's capability to bolster customer service and sales operations. By harnessing predictive analytics and personalized insights, T-Mobile saw notable gains in lead conversion rates and customer satisfaction. The integration of AI allowed for tailored customer interactions, demonstrating how intelligent systems can enhance human decision-making and relationship management.

HubSpot's collaboration with Teamwork.com further exemplifies the advantages of AI in a business context. Initially grappling with pipeline visibility issues, Teamwork.com transitioned to HubSpot, strikingly boosting their sales team's effectiveness by 50%. Automating tedious processes through AI freed up significant time for strategic initiatives, showcasing the dual benefit of operational efficiency and strategic focus.

In presenting these transformations, it's clear that AI is not just a tool but a catalyst for change within sales dynamics. Each instance highlights unique facets of AI capabilities— whether it's enhancing training protocols, refining customer interactions, or optimizing operational workflows. As AI continues to evolve, its role in reshaping sales strategies must be closely monitored and analyzed.

When incorporating AI into sales, practitioners should consider guidelines that ensure effective measurement and attribution of improvements. First, establish clear baseline metrics pre- implementation to facilitate accurate comparisons post-deployment. Second, controlled experiments should be employed to discern AI's specific contributions by isolating variables and focusing on causal relationships. Lastly, actively seek out and integrate customer feedback to understand experiential impacts beyond mere numbers.

Feedback Loop and Continuous Improvement

In today's fast-paced business environment, leveraging AI in sales has become essential. Yet, to truly harness the power of AI, one must focus on establishing continuous feedback loops as part of the sales strategy. These feedback mechanisms are vital for optimizing AI processes and ensuring that technology keeps pace with evolving market demands.

Feedback mechanisms can be integrated effectively into the sales process by incorporating surveys and real-time interactions. Surveys offer structured insights from both customers and sales teams, providing valuable data points for enhancing AI applications. For instance, customer satisfaction surveys can reveal pain points in the sales funnel, allowing AI models to adjust their algorithms to improve user experience. Similarly, surveying sales teams helps identify operational bottlenecks or areas where AI could streamline workflow, ultimately increasing productivity.

Interactions, whether through direct communication channels or automated systems, further enrich this feedback loop. Encouraging customers to share experiences directly or through digital touchpoints creates an ongoing dialogue. This continuous flow of information enables businesses to gauge customer sentiment, aligning AI outputs more closely with customer expectations. It's not merely about gathering feedback but about creating interactive experiences that adapt based on real-time data inputs.

While gathering feedback is crucial, the effectiveness of these mechanisms hinges on the adaptability of AI systems. Adaptive AI models are designed to iterate and evolve based on the feedback they receive, continuously refining their processes to meet specific needs. These models learn from the data collected, identifying trends and patterns which might otherwise be overlooked. For example, an adaptive AI might notice a recurring issue reported by a subset of users and proactively adjust its functions to address it. This adaptability ensures that AI remains responsive and relevant, providing tailored solutions that drive better outcomes in sales operations.

Creating a culture of continuous improvement is equally important. Organizations must foster an environment where open communication and leadership play a pivotal role in encouraging feedback sharing. When all members of the team, from entry-level sales personnel to senior executives, feel empowered to contribute feedback and ideas, it sets a foundation for iterative development and innovation. Leadership must actively promote this culture by establishing clear communication channels and making transparency a priority. Regular workshops and training sessions focused on continuous improvement can equip teams with the skills necessary to engage constructively in feedback-oriented processes.

Moreover, fostering such a culture involves promoting a mindset where change is not only accepted but welcomed. Sales teams need to embrace the perspective that every piece of feedback is an opportunity for growth. When employees understand the value of their input and see tangible improvements resulting from it, they're more likely to engage with and support the AI-driven processes. In turn, this engagement leads to more robust AI integrations that benefit from diverse perspectives across the organization.

Regular iterative evaluations are critical in maintaining agility and responsiveness within AI- driven sales strategies. These assessments allow organizations to review the efficiency and effectiveness of implemented AI solutions, making adjustments as required to align with current objectives and market conditions. Such evaluations should happen at set intervals, but there should also be room for ad-hoc reviews prompted by sudden market dynamics or customer behavior changes.

Iterative reviews involve systematic performance metrics analysis derived from qualitative and quantitative data. Metrics might include conversion rates, customer engagement levels, or sales cycle times. By examining these metrics over time, businesses can recognize shifts or anomalies, providing vital insights into how well the AI systems are performing. Beyond raw numbers, qualitative feedback from team members and users elucidates the broader impact of AI applications on the sales experience.

Importantly, these reviews are not just about identifying what's working well; they're a chance to pinpoint weaknesses and opportunities for enhancement. Suppose a particular feature isn't delivering expected results — rather than assuming it's ineffective, an iterative evaluation encourages deeper investigation into underlying causes and potential redesigns. The goal is to ensure that every component of the

AI system contributes to overarching sales targets, adjusting strategies as needed to optimize outcomes continually.

Insights and Implications

In this chapter, we've delved into the crucial strategies for assessing the outcomes of AI integrations within sales procedures. Sales professionals can effectively measure success and make informed adjustments by establishing key performance indicators (KPIs) tailored to AI applications. It is essential to understand that choosing the right KPIs demands a deep understanding of business objectives and the specific AI technology in use. Aligning these metrics with overarching sales goals ensures that the integration of AI not only meets immediate targets but also supports long-term growth strategies. Distinguishing between traditional sales metrics and those specific to AI initiatives gives companies a clearer view of AI's impact, helping them identify areas for further refinement or enhancement.

Additionally, this chapter has highlighted the importance of integrating both AI-centric and traditional KPIs into existing frameworks, allowing businesses to track short-term results and understand long-term implications comprehensively. By setting quantifiable targets, businesses can maintain focus and track progress over time, establishing benchmarks against industry standards to remain competitive. Furthermore, we've explored the value of collecting feedback from both customers and sales teams, which serves as an indirect measure of AI-driven improvements. Real-world examples have demonstrated how organizations successfully harnessed AI to enhance training protocols, customer interactions, and operational workflows. Such insights guide sales and marketing professionals in effectively implementing AI to drive business growth.

Chapter 10

Real-World Applications and Interviews

E xploring the real-world applications of artificial intelligence in sales is an intriguing journey through the successes and insights gained by industry leaders. These individuals have not only embraced AI but have also transformed their business processes to achieve remarkable outcomes. This chapter showcases the innovative ways executives from various sectors have successfully integrated AI into their sales operations, revolutionizing how they engage with customers and optimize their resources. The narratives from different industries provide a detailed understanding of how AI can become a crucial element for driving sales growth and enhancing customer experiences, urging professionals to consider AI as more than just a technological trend.

Within this chapter, you will encounter compelling case studies that highlight the dynamic role A I plays in reshaping sales strategies. Through interviews with top executives, you will learn about the significant changes AI has brought to lead scoring, customer personalization, and risk assessment. The chapter delves into the importance of maintaining high data quality and ethical considerations when implementing AI solutions. It also examines how personalized marketing and seamless cross-channel integration are benefitting businesses thanks to AI's advanced capabilities. Readers will gain valuable insights into the practical aspects of using AI effectively and ethically in sales, equipping them with knowledge to foster innovation and adapt to evolving market demands.

Profiles of Leaders Successfully Using AI

In today's rapidly evolving business landscape, industry leaders are harnessing the power of artificial intelligence (AI) to redefine sales success. This cutting-edge technology is not merely an accessory but a fundamental driver for innovation and efficiency across sectors. The insights shared by top executives show that AI has emerged as a pivotal tool in transforming traditional sales processes into dynamic strategies capable of generating substantial results.

One striking example comes from a tech company CEO who implemented AI for lead scoring. This process involves evaluating and categorizing potential customers based on their readiness to purchase, thereby enabling tailored engagement strategies. Lead scoring, powered by AI, allows companies to prioritize prospects more accurately, ensuring resources are allocated efficiently. A crucial lesson from this executive's endeavor is the significance of data quality. Without accurate and comprehensive data, even the most sophisticated AI models cannot yield useful predictions. Reliable and clean data serves as the backbone of successful AI applications, reinforcing the need for consistent data management practices in organizations aiming to incorporate advanced technologies.

Switching gears to the retail sector, another executive underscores the transformative impact of AI on customer personalization. This leader has effectively boosted sales conversion rates by integrating AI tools into their sales strategy through targeted recommendations. Personalized experiences are cultivated by analyzing extensive datasets that include browsing history, purchase patterns, and customer preferences. Through machine learning algorithms, AI can predict what customers might want before they know it themselves, crafting individual experiences that significantly enhance engagement and satisfaction. The outcome is a mutually beneficial relationship where customers feel understood and valued, and businesses experience increased loyalty and revenue.

Moreover, AI's influence extends beyond mere transactional interactions; it's redefining the way financial services approach risk assessment. A financial services executive demonstrates how AI can assess client risk profiles with unprecedented precision. Traditionally, risk assessment relied heavily on human judgment and generic criteria, which occasionally led to biased or incomplete evaluations. However, with AI, vast amounts of data can be processed swiftly and without prejudice, resulting in more nuanced and equitable assessments. This practice does not only streamline operations but also plays a critical role in retaining clients by ensuring fair treatment and personalized service offerings. Additionally, ethical considerations have come to the forefront, reminding businesses of the importance of balancing technological advancements with responsibility and transparency.

The stories of these leaders highlight the integral role AI plays in enhancing sales operations while underscoring the often-overlooked facets intrinsic to its execution. From ensuring data integrity and accuracy to fostering rich, personalized customer interactions and promoting equity through unbiased data analysis, each example showcases a piece of the multifaceted relationship between AI and sales success. While challenges such as data privacy and algorithmic bias remain relevant concerns, the strategic adoption of AI offers indisputable advantages that can lead to sustained growth and competitive differentiation.

Companies must adopt proactive approaches towards AI integration to capitalise on these benefits. This starts with cultivating a culture that embraces change and innovation, encouraging teams to continuously explore and adapt to new technological possibilities. Having clear objectives and measurable outcomes helps firms track progress and make necessary adjustments along the way. Ultimately, AI should not be viewed solely as a technological investment but as a means to drive holistic transformation within the organization.

Insights and Lessons from Industry Experts

Incorporating artificial intelligence into sales strategies offers vast potential but also introduces several challenges. To navigate these complexities, insights from industry experts provide valuable guidance on both the benefits and potential pitfalls of AI integration.

Firstly, integrating AI ethically is crucial for organizations aiming to avoid bias in their systems. An AI ethics expert stresses the importance of establishing robust ethical frameworks that guide AI development and application. These frameworks are designed to prevent the unintentional perpetuation of biases, which can skew results and affect customer interactions adversely. Employing an ethics committee within a company can help identify and mitigate potential biases before they become problematic, ensuring AI applications promote fairness and transparency. This approach not only helps in maintaining trust with customers but also aligns with legal and regulatory standards.

Professional development and training are pivotal as AI continues to evolve. A consultant points out that companies must invest in continuous learning opportunities for their staff to keep pace with AI advancements. This involves educating employees about new AI tools and processes regularly through workshops and training sessions, fostering an adaptable workforce. Additionally, selecting user-friendly AI tools simplifies onboarding processes, empowering employees to leverage AI technology effectively without getting overwhelmed. Companies adopting this practice can enhance productivity and ensure smoother transitions when implementing new technologies.

Emerging trends in personalized marketing represent another significant area where AI is reshaping sales strategies. A futurist highlights how AI-driven personalization allows businesses to tailor their marketing efforts more precisely than ever before. AI analyzes customer data, including purchase history and online behavior, to craft personalized incentives and recommendations. As a result, businesses can deliver targeted marketing messages that resonate with individual preferences, ultimately improving engagement and conversion rates. Staying ahead of such technological changes requires openness to experimentation and a strong commitment to ongoing trend analysis, ensuring that strategies remain relevant and effective in dynamic markets.

Finally, seamless cross-channel integration is becoming increasingly important. According to a cross-channel integration expert, aligning AI usage across different sales and marketing channels improves brand consistency and customer experience. This entails using AI to synchronize data and maintain uniform messaging across platforms, whether in email campaigns, social media advertisements, or in-store promotions. The cohesive branding facilitated by AI helps establish a unified brand identity, enabling customers to recognize and engage with the brand effortlessly. Implementing this strategy requires collaboration between sales, marketing, and IT teams to ensure all systems work harmoniously together.

Documenting Case Studies Across Sectors

In today's dynamic business landscape, leveraging AI technology has become not just a strategy but a necessity for industries aiming to optimize their operations and achieve better results. This section presents varied case studies from different sectors, illustrating the real-world applications of AI that are transforming industries and driving growth.

Starting with the automotive industry, AI-driven inventory optimization is revolutionizing how companies manage their stock. Traditionally, managing vehicle inventory posed numerous challenges due to fluctuating demands and long lead times. However, AI now enables businesses to predict demand more accurately, optimize supply chain processes, and make informed decisions regarding production schedules. For instance, advanced algorithms analyze historical sales data, market trends, and even economic indicators to forecast demand precisely, thereby reducing holding costs significantly. By doing so, manufacturers can ensure that the right vehicles are available at the right time, minimizing overstocking and understocking issues. Moreover, enhanced decision-making capabilities allow firms to allocate resources more efficiently, ultimately improving profitability and customer satisfaction in the automotive sector.

Next, we turn our attention to the e-commerce industry, which has seen substantial improvements in customer service through AI chatbots. As online shopping continues to grow, consumer expectations for quick and efficient service have risen. AI- powered chatbots provide a solution by handling high volumes of customer queries simultaneously, offering immediate responses regardless of time zones. These virtual assistants can assist users in navigating websites, answering common questions, guiding product searches, and helping with returns or exchanges. They not only save time for both customers and businesses but also enhance satisfaction by providing a seamless shopping experience. In addition, by collecting and analyzing customer interaction data, AI systems can tailor future communications, further personalizing the customer journey and driving conversion rates.

AI's impact on healthcare services is equally transformative, particularly in streamlining patient lead-generation processes. The healthcare industry often grapples with the challenge of efficiently reaching potential patients who require specific services. Here, AI comes into play by analyzing demographic data, social media activity, and search engine behavior to pinpoint individuals most likely to benefit from particular health offerings. This targeted approach increases the effectiveness of outreach campaigns and results in higher booking rates for healthcare providers. By automating these aspects, medical facilities can focus on delivering quality care while optimizing their marketing efforts. Furthermore, AI systems help refine outreach tactics by continually learning from past interactions, ensuring higher precision and engagement.

Real estate is another sector where AI is making significant strides, particularly in predicting market trends. Real estate agents rely heavily on accurate forecasts to advise clients on buying or selling properties. With AI, agents can analyze vast amounts of historical data, current market conditions, and economic factors to generate predictions about property values and market shifts. This data-driven approach enables agents to offer more informed advice, improving closing rates and fostering stronger client relationships. Additionally, AI facilitates collaboration among stakeholders by providing a unified platform for sharing insights and strategies, promoting coherence and efficiency within teams.

Companies must follow structured action plans to effectively integrate AI into business operations. Identifying AI needs is crucial; organizations should assess specific pain points and determine areas where AI can provide the most value. This requires cross-functional collaboration to establish clear goals and outcomes. Once the needs are identified, implementing AI insights becomes the next step. Businesses need to develop tailored solutions that align with their strategic objectives, often requiring partnerships with AI specialists or investment in training programs. Monitoring progress is essential to ensure that AI initiatives deliver the expected benefits. Regular evaluations and adjustments based on performance metrics can help fine-tune processes for optimal results.

Moreover, fostering an AI-ready culture within the organization is vital for successful implementation. This involves cultivating an environment that welcomes technological advancements and encourages continuous learning. Employees should be provided with adequate resources and training to adapt to new AI tools, mitigating fears of job displacement and highlighting AI as a tool for enhancement rather than replacement. Leadership plays a key role in promoting a positive attitude towards AI, emphasizing its potential to drive innovation and improve overall work experiences.

Final Insights

In this chapter, we explored the experiences of industry leaders who have successfully integrated AI into their sales processes, demonstrating its transformative impact. From enhancing lead scoring in tech companies to boosting customer personalization in retail, these examples illustrate how AI is reshaping traditional sales strategies into more efficient and dynamic systems. By utilizing AI for accurate risk assessment in financial services and personalized marketing efforts, companies are not only improving operational efficiency but also fostering stronger customer relationships. These real-world applications highlight the critical role of data quality and ethical considerations, encouraging organizations to maintain integrity and transparency while adopting AI technologies.

The insights shared emphasize that embracing AI requires a proactive approach and a supportive organizational culture. Companies must invest in continuous learning and professional development to keep up with technological advancements. As AI continues to evolve, businesses should focus on creating cohesive cross-channel integration and leveraging AI-driven personalization to stay competitive. Organizations can harness AI's potential to drive sustainable growth and innovation through strategic adoption and ethical frameworks. Ultimately, this chapter underscores the importance of aligning AI implementation with clear objectives and ongoing evaluation to realize its full benefits in sales and marketing operations.

The Future of Sales—
Intelligently Human

As we look toward the future, one thing is certain: artificial intelligence is not just transforming sales—it is completely redefining the way we sell, engage, and connect with customers. The next chapter in the evolution of sales is already being written, and AI is at the heart of this transformation.

In the years ahead, AI will shift from being a tool for efficiency to becoming a dynamic, integral partner that reshapes every aspect of the sales journey. Sales teams will no longer just rely on AI to automate tasks or analyze data—they will co-evolve with it, leveraging its predictive power and real-time insights to drive smarter decisions and create deeper connections with customers. From the first touchpoint to post-sale engagement, AI will power hyper-personalized experiences, anticipating customer needs and preferences before they are even articulated.

The true magic of this future will lie in the way AI amplifies the *human* aspects of sales. With repetitive tasks automated and data-driven insights delivered instantly, sales professionals will be freed to focus on what they do best: building trust, fostering relationships, and understanding the complex emotions that drive human buying decisions. In this new world, AI will give salespeople superhuman capabilities to create experiences that are not only efficient but deeply resonant—tailored to each customer's unique desires, needs, and aspirations.

Imagine a sales ecosystem where every interaction is not just a transaction but an opportunity to create a lasting, meaningful connection. AI will enable sales teams to personalize experiences at a level of granularity that was once unimaginable, while also optimizing the entire sales process for maximum impact. It won't just be about closing deals—it will be about creating long-term value, nurturing relationships, and fostering customer loyalty in ways that were previously out of reach.

This vision for the future of sales is not just about automation; it's about *intelligence*—intelligent systems that understand the customer journey, adapt in real-time to shifting needs, and empower sales teams to deliver exceptional, customized experiences at scale. The future of sales will be a world where AI augments human capabilities, allowing sales professionals to connect with customers in ways that feel both deeply personal and hyper-intelligent.

As we stand on the cusp of this revolution, the possibilities are endless. AI will continue to evolve, and with it, the very nature of sales will transform. Those who embrace this change will be the leaders of tomorrow—driving growth, innovation, and customer loyalty in ways that blur the lines between technology and humanity.

In the end, the future of sales isn't just automated—it's intelligently *human*. And as AI continues to reshape the way we do business, it will open up a world of opportunities that were once confined to the realm of imagination.

About the Author

Lionel Sim is an AI strategist, entrepreneur, and thought leader, recognized for his ability to help organizations leverage artificial intelligence to drive transformative business outcomes. With over a decade of hands-on experience in digital marketing, digital transformation, and strategic innovation, Lionel has advised and partnered with companies across industries—from agile startups to global enterprises—helping them navigate the rapidly changing landscape of technology to achieve sustained growth, operational excellence, and a competitive edge.

In The AI Selling Revolution, Lionel distills his extensive expertise into a powerful resource for business leaders and innovators. The book provides a roadmap for integrating AI into business strategy, showcasing how AI can be used not just as a tool, but as a fundamental driver of business success in an increasingly competitive and automated world. Drawing on his years of experience, Lionel offers readers actionable insights, practical frameworks, and real-world examples of how to make AI a key differentiator in today's fast-paced marketplace.

A sought-after speaker and advisor, Lionel is known for his ability to simplify complex AI concepts and translate them into strategic actions that create tangible value for businesses. He is passionate about advocating for the ethical and responsible use of AI and is committed to empowering organizations to build AI solutions that benefit both their bottom line and society as a whole.

Outside of his consulting work and writing, Lionel dedicates his time to mentoring emerging technologists and entrepreneurs, speaking at industry events, and contributing to the ongoing conversation around the future of AI. His work continues to inspire a new generation of leaders who are ready to harness the power of AI to shape the future of business and society.

Reference

Chapter 1

Advanced Analytics Techniques: How AI Transforms Lead Scoring for Event Marketers! - momencio. (2024, May 15). Momencio. https:// www.momencio.com/advanced-analytics- techniques-AI-lead-scoring/

Kannan, N., & Research Scholar II. (2024, February 22). *AI-Enabled Customer Relationship Management in the Financial Industry: A Case Study Approach.* ResearchGate; unknown. https:// www.researchgate.net/publication/378371886_AI-

Enabled_Customer_Relationship_Management_in_the_Fi nancial_Industry_A_Case_Study_Approac h

Paschen, J., Wilson, M., & Ferreira, J. J. (2020, February). *Collaborative intelligence: How human and artificial intelligence create value along the B2B sales funnel.* Business Horizons. https:// doi.org/10.1016/j.bushor.2020.01.003

Sunshine, M. (2024). *The Role of A I in Sales Strategy: Leveraging Predictive Analytics for Smarter*

Targeting. Thecenterforsalesstrategy.com. https://blog.thecenterforsalesstrategy.com/the-role-of-AI- in-sales-strategy

Team, H. (2024, March 14). *The Impact of AI on Sales Strategies and Performance.* Highspot. https://www.highspot.com/blog/AI-sales/

The Impact of AI on Customer Relationship Management: Enhancing Engagement and *Personalisation* | *ProfileTree.* (2024, May 9). ProfileTree Web Design and Digital Marketing. https://profiletree.com/impact-of-AI-on-customer- relationship-management/

Chapter 2

10 Top Sales Analytics Software in 2024 (Features + *Pricing).* (2024). Scratchpad.com. https://www.scratchpad.com/blog/sales-analytics-software

10 Essential Criteria for Evaluating AI Enterprise Search Tools in 2024. (2024, March 6). Dashworks.ai. https://www.dashworks.ai/blog/ the-10-essential-criteria-for-evaluating-AI- enterprise-search-in-2024

AI for Sales Enhancing Strategies and Performance. (2024, October 23). Salesloft.com; Salesloft. https://www.salesloft.com/resources/ blog/AI-for-sales

Bodansky, W. (2024, March 31). AI *Sales Automation: Salesforce Einstein, Hubspot ChatSpot.AI &...* STACK

BD.   https://stackbd.com/   2024/03/31/AI-sales-automation/

https://www.facebook.com/6senseinc. (2024, September 13). *The Skeptic's Guide to Shopping for AI-Powered Tools | 6sense.* 6sense. https:// 6sense.com/guides/shopping-for-AI-powered- tools/insivia. (2024, October 4). AI *Sales Tools & Uses.* Insivia. https://www.insivia.com/AI-sales-tools- uses/

Chapter 3

AI Sales Forecasting in 2024: Your Guide to More Profitable Pipelines.   (2024).   Scratchpad.com. https://www.scratchpad.com/blog/AI-sales- forecasting

AI's Impact on Modern Sales Strategies. (2023). Get1page.com.   https://www.get1page.com/post/AI-impact-modern-sales-strategies

Sjödin, D., Parida, V., Palmié, M., & Wincent, J. (2021, September). *How AI capabilities enable business model innovation: Scaling AI through co-evolutionary processes and feedback loops.* Journal of Business Research. https://doi.org/ 10.1016/j.jbusres.2021.05.009

Takyar, A. (2024, January 23). AI *in sales: Transforming customer engagement and conversion.* LeewayHertz - A I   Development   Company. https://www.leewayhertz.com/AI-in- sales/

Wilson, H. J., & Daugherty, P. R. (2018, July). *Collaborative Intelligence: Humans and AI Are Joining Forces*. Harvard Business Review. https://hbr.org/2018/07/collaborative-intelligence- humans-and-AI-are-joining-forces insivia. (2024, October 4). *Using AI for Sales: Revolutionizing SDRs & BDRs Ability to Achieve Efficiency and Effectiveness*. Insivia. https://www.insivia.com/AI-for-sales-revolutionizing-sdrs- bdrs-ability-to-achieve-efficiency-and- effectiveness/

Chapter 4

Boris. (n.d.). *Predictive Sales Forecasting: What You Need to Know*. Www.getweflow.com. https://www.getweflow.com/blog/predictive-sales- forecasting

Ballard, J. (n.d.). *Importance Of Personalized Customer Experience And Ways To Achieve It*. Paradox Marketing. https://paradoxmarketing.io/capabilities/crm-strategy/insights/importance-of-personalized-customer-experience-and-ways-to- achieve-it/

Brenner, M. (2023, December 13). *Content Marketing Personalization Strategies to Make Customers Love You*. Marketing Insider Group. https://marketinginsidergroup.com/content-marketing/content-marketing-personalization-strategies/

Staff, S. (2024, June 25). *What is Big Data, and Why Does it Matter?* Salesforce. https://www.salesforce.com/au/blog/big-data/

What is Big Data Analytics? Definition, Benefits, and Use-cases. (n.d.). ThoughtSpot. https://www.thoughtspot.com/data-trends/analytics/big- data-analytics https://www.facebook.com/6senseinc. (2024). *How to Use Predictive Sales Forecasting in 2024 | 6sense.* 6sense. https://6sense.com/platform/ predictive-analytics/predictive-sales-forecasting/

Chapter 5

AI for Lead Generation: How it Works + Useful Tools. (2024). IOVOX. https://www.iovox.com/ blog/AI-lead-generation

Allen, J. (2021). *How AI SDRs Can 10x Your Sales Team's Productivity.* Tbtech.co. https://tbtech.co/ news/how-AI-sdrs-can-10x-your-sales-teams- productivity/

Finn, T., & Downie, A. (2024, July 11). AI *in CRM (Customer Relationship Management) | IBM.* Www.ibm.com. https://www.ibm.com/think/ topics/AI-crm

Praburam. (2024, July 12). *How to Automate Repetitive Tasks.* ClickUp. https://clickup.com/ blog/automate-repetitive-tasks/

Supercharge Your Sales Pipeline: How AI Optimizes Every Stage. (2022). 11sight.com. https://www.11sight.com/technology/supercharge- your-sales-pipeline-how-AI-optimizes-every-stage

Top 6 AI Powered CRMs + How to Use Them in 2025. (2024). Scratchpad.com. https://www.scratchpad.com/blog/AI-crm

Chapter 6

AI Transparency: Building Trust in AI. (n.d.). Mailchimp. https://mailchimp.com/resources/AI- transparency/

Author, G. (2023, March 30). *Customer Data Privacy: 10 Non-Negotiable Best Practices to Protect Your Business.* WordStream. https://www.wordstream.com/blog/ws/2022/11/22/ customer-data-privacy

Customer Privacy and Consent Best Practices. (n.d.). Www.pingidentity.com. https://www.pingidentity.com/en/resources/blog/post/customer-privacy-and-consent-best-practices.html

Ferrara, E. (2023, December 26). *Fairness and Bias in Artificial Intelligence: A Brief Survey of Sources, Impacts, and Mitigation Strategies.* Sci; Multidisciplinary Digital Publishing Institute. https://doi.org/10.3390/sci6010003

Varsha, P. S. (2023, April). *How can we manage biases in artificial intelligence systems – A systematic literature review.* International Journal of Information Management Data Insights. https://doi.org/10.1016/j.jjimei.2023.100165

Wren, H. (2024, January 18). *What is AI transparency? A comprehensive guide.* Zendesk. https://www.zendesk.com/blog/AI-transparency/

Chapter 7

Deeb, G. (n.d.). *Artificial Intelligence Is Revolutionizing Sales Coaching.* Forbes.https://www.forbes.com/sites/georgedeeb/2023/12/04/artificial-intelligence-is-revolutionizing-sales-coaching/

Fuchs, J. (2024, October 2). *How to Train (& Onboard) Your Sales Team With AI.* Hubspot.com; HubSpot. https://blog.hubspot.com/ sales/AI-training-fo-sales

How AI can help train sales teams (and where it can slow them down). (2024). Outreach. https://www.outreach.io/resources/blog/AI-sales-training

Haleem, A., Javaid, M., Qadri, M. A., & Suman, R. (2022). *Understanding the role of digital technologies in education: A review.* Sustainable Operations and

Computers. https://doi.org/ 10.1016/j.susoc.2022.05.004

Movchan, S. (2018). *What Makes a Good Learning Environment.* Raccoongang.com. https:// raccoongang.com/blog/what-makes-good-learning-environment/

SellingPower.com. (2024). Sellingpower.com. https://www.sellingpower.com/22061/the-key-to-success-with-AI-driven-learning-and-development

Chapter 8

AI-Powered Upselling & Cross-Selling: 2024 Guide. (2024, May 12). Dialzara.com. https:// dialzara.com/blog/AI-powered-upselling-and-cross- selling-2024-guide/

Gupta, A. (2024, July 23). *Emerging Technologies in CRM: The Role of AI, Big Data, and Beyond | CustomerThink.* Customerthink.com. https:// customerthink.com/emerging-technologies-in-crm- the-role-of-AI-big-data-and-beyond/

Maderis, G. (2023, September 11). *5 benefits of using A I chatbots in customer service.* Zendesk. https://www.zendesk.com/blog/5-benefits-using- AI-bots-customer-service/

PWC. (2022). *The Essential Eight Technologies*. PwC. https://www.pwc.com/us/en/tech-effect/ emerging-tech/essential-eight-technologies.html

Rafalski, K. (2023, April 19). Instant Assistance: How AI Chatbots Are Improving Customer Service. www.netguru.com. https://www.netguru.com/ blog/AI-chatbots-improving-customer-service https://kodzilla.pl, & dev@kodzilla.pl. (2019, April 12). *Addepto*. Addepto. https://addepto.com/blog/ up-selling-cross-selling-5-reasons-use-machine- learning/

Chapter 9

Anchia, C. (2024, April 11). *Measuring Success: Key Metrics and KPIs for AI Initiatives*. Acacia Advisors. https://chooseacacia.com/measuring- success-key-metrics-and-kpis-for-AI-initiatives/

Hariguna, T., & Ruangkanjanases, A. (2024, January 1). Assessing the impact of artificial intelligence on customer performance: A quantitative study using partial least squares methodology. Data Science and Management; KeAi. https://doi.org/10.1016/j.dsm.2024.01.001

Schrage, M., Kiron, D., Candelon, F., Khodabandeh, S., & Chu, M. (2023, July 11). *Improve Key Performance Indicators With AI*. MIT Sloan Management Review.

https://sloanreview.mit.edu/ article/improve-key-performance-indicators-with- ai/

Susko, B. (2024, June 13). *The Rise of AI-Powered Sales Tools*. Quantified AI. https:// www.quantified.ai/blog/the-rise-of-AI-powered- sales-tools/

Chapter 10

AI For Business - 30 Case Studies That Led To Competitive Advantage. (2023, March 6). Digitaltransformationskills.com. https:// digitaltransformationskills.com/AI-for-business/

Kolesnikova, I. (2023, August 22). *The Complete Guide to Leveraging AI for Sales in 2023*. MindTitan. https://mindtitan.com/resources/ industry-use-cases/AI-for-sales/

Ledro, C., Nosella, A., & Pozza, I. D. (2023, October 1). *Integration of AI in CRM: Challenges and guidelines*. Journal of Open Innovation: Technology, Market, and Complexity; Springer Science+Business Media. https://doi.org/10.1016/ j.joitmc.2023.100151

Pohrebniyak, I. (2024, April 26). *Generative AI for Customer Experience: 17 Cases from Global Brands*. Master of Code Global. https://masterofcode.com/blog/generative-AI-for-customer-experience

Rane, N., Paramesha, M., Choudhary, S., & Rane, J. (2024, January 1). *Artificial Intelligence in Sales and Marketing: Enhancing Customer Satisfaction, Experience and Loyalty*. Social Science Research Network; RELX Group (Netherlands). https://doi.org/10.2139/ssrn.4831903

Takyar, A. (2019, August 2). AI *Use Cases Major Industries*. LeewayHertz - Software Development Company. https://www.leewayhertz.com/AI-use-cases-and-applications/

www.ingramcontent.com/pod-product-compliance
Lightning Source LLC
LaVergne TN
LVHW051342050326
832903LV00031B/3701